BARCODE ON
NEXT PAGE

Olivier Clément

# YOU ARE PETER

## An Orthodox Theologian's Reflection
## on the Exercise of Papal Primacy

## Kenrick-Glennon
### Seminary Library

Charles L. Souvay Memorial

New City Press
New York   London   Manila

# Foreword

In *Ut unum sint*, his 1995 encyclical on ecumenism, John Paul II boldly placed the exercise of his primatial office on the ecumenical agenda. He asked the leaders and theologians of churches not in union with Rome to engage with him in a patient and fraternal dialogue, seeking "to find a way of exercising the primacy which, while in no way renouncing what is essential to its mission, is nonetheless open to a new situation" (UUS 95).

The numerous responses from leaders and theologians of various ecclesial traditions could be seen as an answer to the prayer of John Paul II to the Holy Spirit "to shine his light upon us, enlightening all the Pastors and theologians of our Churches, that we may seek—together, of course—the forms in which this [petrine] ministry may accomplish a service of love recognized by all concerned" (UUS 95). They exemplify what the Pope called "a dialogue in which, leaving useless controversies behind, we could listen to one another, keeping before us only the will of Christ for his Church and allowing ourselves to be deeply moved by his plea 'that they may all be one . . . so that the world may believe that you have sent me' (Jn 17:21)" (UUS 96). The present work is manifestly inspired by the same irenic attitude.

Olivier Clément is a French-speaking professor at the celebrated Institute of Saint Sergius (*Saint-Serge*) in Paris. That institute, founded by Russian émigré Christians in 1925, became and still remains a thriving center of Orthodox intellectual life in the West. Initially directed by such giants as Nicholas Berdiaev and Serge Boulgakov, it grew to even greater prominence through the contributions of Vladimir Lossky, Nicolas Afanassieff, and Paul Evdokimov. The ecumenical spirit and erudition of Saint Sergius were brought to the United States by theologians of the stature of Georges Florovsky, Alexander Schmemann, and John Meyendorff.

Professor Clément's response to John Paul II first appeared in France under the title *Rome autrement. Un orthodoxe face à la papauté* (Paris: Desclée de Brouwer, 1997). The book, solidly rooted in the Orthodox tradition, represents the cordial and open mentality characteristic of the theologians of Saint Sergius. I would judge that it is almost exactly the kind of response for which Pope John Paul II was hoping. It is a pleasure to be able to present to English-speaking readers this concise, learned, and articulate presentation.

Ecumenical advancement is a slow process, requiring much patience. It took some fourteen centuries for Chalcedonians and non-Chalcedonians to begin to realize that they are fundamentally in agreement about the divinity and humanity of Christ. We may hope that the deep wounds mutually inflicted upon each other by Orthodox and Catholics at the dawn of the second millennium will not take fourteen centuries to heal. In any case, we have the satisfaction of seeing that a process of mutual correction and mutual enrichment is under way. Amid uncertainties and setbacks a healing of memories is at work. Professor Clément's contribution, while quite properly registering a distinctively Orthodox point of view, is a sign of the progress thus far made and a beacon of hope for the future.

Avery Cardinal Dulles, S.J.

# Introduction

The problem of the papacy is clearly the greatest difficulty facing ecumenical dialogue today, and particularly the dialogue between Catholicism and Orthodoxy. Yet there is a doorway of hope. In his encyclical, *Ut unum sint,* John Paul II expressed a desire for common reflection on the exercise of papal primacy. The essay you are about to read is a response to this request. I shall place the emphasis on the history and experience of the undivided Church, before recalling the contrasting developments of eastern and western Christianity and concluding with the tasks that call us to unity.

# Abbreviations

ACO  *Acta Conciliorum Oecumenicorum.* Berlin-Lepzing, 1927.

Denziger  *Enchiridion Symbolorum Definitionum et Declarationum de Rebus Fidei et Morum.* Edited by F. Denzinger. Freiburg im Breisgau: Herder, 1963.

Mansi  *Sacrorum Conciliorum nova ed amplissima collectio.* Edited by G. Mansi. Forence, 1759-1763.

Lumen Gentium  *Documents of the Second Vatican Council.* Edited by Austin Flannery. Northport, NY: Costello Publishing Co., 1996.

PG  *Patrologia cursus completus. Series graeca.* 161 volumes. Edited by J.-P. Migne. Paris, 1857-1866.

PL  *Patrologia cursus completus. Series latina.* 221 volumes. Edited by J.-P. Migne. Paris, 1878-1890.

SC  *Sources Chrétiennes.* Paris: Cerf, 1942-.

# 1.

# An Ecclesiology of Communion

For Christians of the first centuries, as Nicolas Afanassieff[1] and John Zizioulas[2] have aptly demonstrated, there was no ecclesiology *per se*. The early Church, threatened though it was by the sin and betrayal of its members, remained in its depths transparent to the threefold mystery of Christ, the Spirit and the Father, himself the source and foundation of trinitarian communion.

The Church is above all the body of Christ. Scripture culminates in the Incarnation, when God, transcending the context of his word, gave us the Word, so that he might communicate to us his very life, that is to say, the Resurrection. The Church is thus a "place of rebirth," the "mystery of life," "Christ complete in head and body."[3] "Between head and body there is no space at all, the slightest space would kill us."[4] The Church is thus the sacrament, or "mystery" as the East says, of the Risen One who raises us. At the heart of this all-embracing sacramentality, which fulfills and manifests the sacramental character of creation, is the eucharist.

The eucharist is the "mystery of mysteries," of which scripture, read and commented upon in the first part of the liturgical celebration, is henceforth a dimension. It is the eucharist that makes of the Church the body of Christ, for it is through the eucharist that the faithful, as Paul says, are "incorporated" in Christ; hence, through the eucharist, the Church is "in Christ." "And as there is one loaf, so we, although there are many of us, are one single body, for we all share in the one loaf" (1 Cor 10:17).[5]

Thus the church of any given place (which in those days was a city and its surrounding countryside, the administrative unit inherited from the city of antiquity and one, moreover, very ill-adapted to the vast metropolis of today) is, thanks to the apostolic succession of its bishop, not a part or province of the universal Church. Rather, as the *casta meretrix* (chaste prostitute), it both is already and called unceasingly to become a full manifestation of the "one, holy and apostolic" Church, in the words of the creed of Nicaea and Constantinople. Every local church, across space and time, finds its identity in the one body of Christ to whom each bears witness. Their communion is a true eucharistic consubstantiality, guaranteed by an identity of faith and of episcopal ministry, each bishop having the two inseparable missions of presiding over a local church and expressing, through his communion with other bishops, the unity of the universal Church: the particular in the universal and, thereby, the universal in and through the particular. Each church is thus responsible for the others, "receiving" the witness of the others and offering itself in turn to be "received" by them. This continual reciprocity attests that they are, individually and collectively, the Church.

The body of Christ, the Church, is at the same time the temple of the Holy Spirit. The Spirit impregnated the earthly existence of Christ, constituting his messianic anointing, the *sôma pneumatikon* or "spiritual body," according to Paul, penetrated by the energies of the Spirit.

It is in the Spirit that the Church is mystery-of- resurrection. Every sacramental celebration calls down (in what is known as the *epiklesis*) the presence and action of the Spirit, for the Church does not magically possess her Lord.

Moreover, only the *epiklesis* allows the clear expression of the universal priesthood of all the faithful as well as of the ordained priesthood of the bishop and of the presbyters who, due to the sheer number of parishes, have become his delegates. (Why the parishes were not "episcopalized" remains, in my opinion, an enigma and modifies considerably the original role of the bishop, for in practice the eucharistic community was from quite early times none other than the parish.) In the *epiklesis* there is both an invocation and a declaration: everyone takes part in the invocation; the bishop (priest) declares the granting of this request. Thus the laity, who are "bearers of the Spirit" by virtue of their baptism and confirmation, are likewise among those responsible for the truth, especially those spiritually committed who live it more intensely (hence the often decisive role of monks in the history of the Church). They are not in opposition to the episcopacy or the sacramental institution, for they are rooted in its depths (the true prophetic role is sacramental), but they exist in order to purify it and prevent it from becoming its own object; they call it back if need be to its true vocation. For the understanding of the bishops is not a passive factor, there to be acted on by the Spirit; it demands on their part collaboration and sanctification. The encyclical of the eastern patriarchs, in 1848, would specify that the bishops were the "judges" and the faithful the "shields" of the truth, thus extending the fundamental theme of "reception" to the entire people of God. (Significantly, during the early centuries the bishops were elected by the entire diocese, clergy *and* laity.)

It can happen that a council is, in fact, hijacked, as happened at Ephesus in 449 or at Hiereia in 754. The resulting protests and disorder should not be mistaken for democratic consultation: sometimes a single individual, strengthened in conscience by prophetic inspiration, can testify to the truth. Maximus the Confessor, in 658, played such a part in the critical monothelite controversy, which called into question the full reality of human freedom.[6] Sooner or later the prophet is heard by the episcopacy, which is woken by his voice and gives to this seemingly isolated opinion an ecclesial weight, as indeed it did, less than twenty years after the martyrdom of Maximus, at the ecumenical council of 680–681.

As Kallistos Ware emphasizes, "Conciliar decisions are not true because they are accepted by the Church; they are accepted by the Church because they are true."[7] And this "reception" is the sign that the mind of the Church has truly expressed itself through the council.

Because the Church is the body of Christ to which the Spirit gives life, it is "the Father's house." The divine unity does not refer to some neutral essence but to the Person of the Father: "One God because one Father," a "name even greater than that of God."[8] "In an eternal dynamism of love,"[9] the Father, source and principle of divinity, grounds in himself the otherness-oneness of the Son and the Spirit and communicates to them all that he is. By this eternal "beginning," which the Prologue to John's Gospel evokes, "God is love," the source of all love. It can equally be said that he is communion and the source of all communion. Because she is "the Father's house," the Church participates in (and must show that she does so) the trinitarian mode of existence: the Church is a dispensation of trinitarian love at the heart of humanity, of the love and freedom that come from the divine abyss, which itself is freedom and love. The divine life that comes from the Father, through the Son, in the Holy Spirit, gives itself to humanity, calling us to a communion similar to that of the Trinity (but embryonic and ever veiled by our opacity). God exists in three persons, a "meta-mathematical" number, which is beyond number and expresses complete unity in complete diversity (and vice versa). Under the breath and fire of the Spirit, there exists in Christ a single human Being in a multitude of persons: the body of Christ in which we are all "members of one another." Each person, in this same unity, is personally received by Christ; each is consecrated by a Pentecostal flame in his or her unique vocation.

This communion, whose source is the Father, grounds the Spirit-dimension of the Church, the convergence and, ultimately, harmony of personal consciences, which become the guardians of a Truth that is love. This communion also grounds her properly christological dimension, the communion of the local churches, that is to say, her permanent conciliarity. It is moreover traditional that every bishop be consecrated by three bishops of neighboring dioceses or "eparchies." From the beginning, his ministry is situated in episcopal collegiality.

From early on, to avert potential isolation or conflict between local communities, and to help them in times of crisis beyond their solution, some of the more prestigious churches, often those of apostolic origin, found themselves invested with a more generally recognized capacity for "receiving" and therefore for "solicitude." Thus, there developed an entire hierarchy of centers of dialogue or primacies: major centers endowed with certain privileges (*presbeia*) and mentioned by the first ecumenical councils

(Rome, Alexandria, Antioch). From the fifth century on they became known as "patriarchates." Because of its importance as the new capital of the empire, "the other Rome" (*altera Roma*), Constantinople, was to join them, and ecclesial communion then took the form of a "Pentarchy" (Rome, Constantinople, Alexandria, Antioch, Jerusalem). As a general rule, the primate enjoyed the right of appeal and confirmed the consecration of bishops. The "solicitude" of these five sees, and especially that of Rome and Constantinople, covered the entire Church. The thirty-fourth canon, so-called "apostolic," which in reality seems to go back to the third century (the period when the metropolitan provinces were being formed), aptly expresses the spirit of these "primacies": "It is fitting that the bishops of each people (*ethnos*) should know who is first among them, that they should acknowledge him as head and not undertake anything beyond the confines of their own sees without having consulted him. But the one who is first, for his part, must not do anything without consulting them. Thus a communion of thought will reign, and God will be glorified in the Lord (the Christ) through the Holy Spirit." The trinitarian reference is significant. The Roman affirmation of a primacy that corresponds to a particular charism roots itself here.

## Notes

1. Nicolas Afanassieff, *L'Église du Saint Esprit* (Paris, 1975).
2. John Zizioulas, *L'être ecclésial* (Geneva, 1981).
3. Augustine, *In Joannis Evangelium*, XXVIII, PL 35, 1622.
4. John Chrysostom, *In Epistolam I ad Corinthos, Homilia VIII*, PG 61, 72.
5. Unless otherwise noted, all biblical citations are from the New Jerusalem Bible (trans.).

6. The doctrine according to which Christ had only a divine will.

7. Kallistos Ware, "L'exercice de l'autorité dans l'Église orthodoxe," *Irénikon* 54 (1981): 451–471 at 469.

8. Cyril of Alexandria, *Thesaurus de Sancta et Consubstantiali Trinitate*, PG 75, 65.

9. Maximus the Confessor, *Scholia in librum de Divinis Nominibus*, PG 4, 221 A.

# 2.

# Peter and Paul, Martyrs

From as early as the first century the local church of Rome enjoyed particular prestige because of the presence of the bodies and burial places of the two apostles Peter and Paul, who brought to Rome the supreme witness of martyrdom. Their witness is the foundation of the witness of the Church, which celebrates the eucharist on the site of their "confession."

There is a close connection between the confession of faith and martyrdom. The Second Letter to Timothy has Paul saying that he has "kept the faith" and that his "life is already being poured away as a libation" (2 Tim 4:6–7). When Jesus says to Peter at the end of John's Gospel, "Feed my sheep," he also tells him that he will "stretch out his hands" and that "somebody else" will take him where he "would rather not go" (Jn 21:18). A passage from Irenaeus on the "most powerful origin" of the church of Rome is famous. It concerns, he says, "the great church, the best known and the most ancient of all churches, founded and constituted by the two glorious apostles Peter and Paul...." Because of this "most powerful origin—*propter potentiorem principalitatem*," to be in accord with this church is a guarantee of accord with the gospel faith. Accord with other prestigious sees would render the same service, he adds, but the priority of Rome's reception and witness is more radiant and, in a certain sense, more central, more easily accessible.[1]

The joint commemoration of the apostles Peter and Paul is attested to at Rome from the second half of the third century. The feast was soon found in the East, which celebrated on June 29 these "princes of the apostles and universal doctors," these "chorus leaders," this "dyad of the Trinity," yet without opening the least rift between them and the college of apostles as a whole, for June 30 was consecrated to the "*synaxis* (assembly) of the twelve glorious and illustrious apostles." The entire New Testament bears witness to the importance of Peter and Paul, the first part of the Acts of the Apostles being built around the testimony of Peter, the second part around Paul's.

The gospel emphasizes over and again the place of Peter as first among the twelve. "Simon and his companions," we read (Mk 1:36); and again, "Peter stood up with the Eleven," or "Peter and the other apostles" (Acts 2:14 and 37). Peter is first on the list of apostles; he is the first to confess Jesus as Messiah; the first to see the risen Christ. It is Peter who gives Pentecost its orientation and from then on becomes the spokesman for the infant Church. In the name of the other apostles he proclaims the fundamental message: "God raised this man Jesus to life, and of that we are all witnesses" (Acts 2:32).

This *prôtos*, for all that, does not stand alone. *Prôtos* means the first in a series and not *arché*, the first cause, for that could only be Christ. The other apostles—and the prophets, as Paul interestingly adds—are, along with Peter, "the foundations" of the Church, "and Christ Jesus himself is the cornerstone" (Eph 2:20). They too receive the power to bind and loose, that is to say, according to the meaning these words had in the Judaism of the day, whether or not to reintegrate a person into the community (Jn 10:23), and James, the brother of John, is the first martyr-apostle (Acts 12:2).

The *prôtos* does not absorb the others. His opinion carries weight at the "council" of Jerusalem but is not decisive. James, "the apostles and elders and the whole church" (Acts 2:23) all have their roles; they situate Peter within a communion. Hence, Peter is the "first," but if he is called to "strengthen" his brothers, it is not up to him to establish or justify their ministry; that comes directly from Christ, as is made clear in the calling of Paul, recognized but not deter-mined by Peter.

Three statements of Christ define Peter's role: "You are Peter and on this rock I will build my community" (Mt 16:18); "and once you have recovered, you in your turn must strengthen your brothers" (Lk 22:32); "Simon . . . do you love me more than these others do? . . . Feed my sheep" (Jn 21:15–17). Now the first point to make is that all three are situated in a resurrection and eucharistic context. According to the tradition of the early Church, the true celebration of the eucharist is the basis for the ecclesiality of the local church and for its connection with *all the churches*.

The second point is that two of these statements are almost immediately followed by very stern warnings. When, on the basis of Peter's confession of faith, Jesus establishes him as the rock on which he will build his Church, Peter refuses to accept that this Messiah, whom he has just proclaimed, is identical with the Suffering Servant. Whereupon Jesus flings at him: "Get behind me, Satan! You are an obstacle in my path, because you are thinking not as God thinks but as human beings do" (Lk 16:23). And when Jesus says to Peter (Lk 22:32), "I have prayed for you,

Simon, that your faith may not fail, and once you have recovered, you in your turn must strengthen your brothers," and Peter announces impetuously that he is ready to share the destiny of his master, Jesus responds: "I tell you, Peter, by the time the cock crows today you will have denied three times that you know me" (Lk 22:34).

The third remark, at the end of John's Gospel, shows that Peter, if he wants to be faithful to his calling, must be the very example of the pardoned sinner. After reinstating Peter as first among the apostles ("Do you love me more than the others?"), Christ warns him again and promises him nothing else than martyrdom.

The presence of Peter in the Church—we will show in the following chapter how this presence can manifest itself— has thus no connection at all with worldly glory: it can do nothing but remind the Church that it draws its life from God's forgiveness and has no other power than that of the cross.

Christ himself rejected the temptation of earthly power; he refused to be made a king; it was by death that he conquered death; he rose unseen and revealed himself only in response to love. And he taught his disciples, "Among the gentiles it is the kings who lord it over them, and those who have authority over them are given the title Benefactor. With you this must not happen. No; the greatest among you must behave as if he were the youngest, the leader as if he were the one who serves" (Lk 22:25–26).

If there is something of the institution in Peter's role, Paul appears as the charismatic apostle. His call is proof that grace can bypass institutions, since he, Paul—the "child untimely born," the erstwhile persecutor of the Church—was made an apostle alongside, as it were, the newly reconstituted structure of the Twelve. Yet he is utterly convinced that his preaching of the gospel is as important as Peter's. Peter's first mission—and a noble mission it is—is to the Chosen People, that they might recognize their Messiah. Paul receives the Son's revelation "that I should preach him to the gentiles. I was in no hurry to confer with any human being, or to go up to Jerusalem to see those who were already apostles before me. Instead, I went off . . . " (Gal 1:16–17). It is only after three years that he comes to Jerusalem to meet Peter and James, "the brother of the Lord." It is fourteen years later that he comes back, this time addressing "the recognized leaders" (Gal 2:2), the pillars of the Church, and making them acknowledge his vocation. Nor does he hesitate to oppose Peter when the latter capitulates before the demands of the Jewish Christians that he stop taking meals with the gentiles. "However, when Cephas came to Antioch," the very place where Christianity was making contact with the wider world, "then did I oppose him to his face since he was manifestly wrong" and "their behavior was not true to the gospel" (Gal 2:11 and 14). To want to impose the prescriptions of the Law, beginning with circumcision, on gentile converts removes the stumbling-block of the cross (Gal 5:11). As we know, the controversy was not settled by Peter, repentant in fact of his faint-heartedness, but by the first council. And when the community of Corinth splits up, some declaring for Paul, others for Peter or Apollos, and still others (how ironic!) "for Christ" (1 Cor 1:12), Paul will have no human reference made, no more to Peter than to himself, proclaiming that the only foundation is Christ. "So there is to be no boasting about human beings: everything belongs to you, whether it is Paul, or Apollos, or Cephas, the world, life or death, the present or the future—all belong to you; but you belong to Christ and Christ belongs to God" (1 Cor 3:21–23).

Peter and Paul or, in other words, the first and the last of the apostles, came to Rome, to the capital of the empire, where all idolatry was concentrated, "Babylon the Great, the mother of . . . all the filthy practices on the earth" (Rv 17:5), for it was there that Christ's victory over all forms of death must be proclaimed. As martyrs—seized, that is to say, by the Resurrection—they are for ever present in Rome. This is how the early Church understood it, not as a question of succession to be discussed. Peter and Paul "live and preside" in the church of Rome.[2] It is the place "where the apostles (Peter and Paul) preside daily and where their blood renders constant testimony to the glory of God."

There is, moreover, in the role of Peter—more than in Paul's—something which cannot be handed on. He is one of the Twelve who can have no successors to the unique character of their witness: having lived with Jesus, then having encountered the risen One, they attest to the radical unity of the "Jesus of history" and the "Christ of faith," to borrow an expression from contemporary exegesis. Peter himself expressed it quite clearly when it was necessary to replace Judas and rebuild the college of apostles: "Out of the men who have been with us the whole time that the Lord Jesus was living with us, from the time when John was baptizing until the day when he was taken up from us, one must be appointed to serve with us as a witness to his resurrection" (Acts 1:21–22).

Paul, on the other hand, never knew Jesus "according to the flesh." He saw/heard Christ glorified. Moreover, he was the first of those whom the orthodox Church calls "apostolic men," who, concentrating within themselves to combustion point the apostolic nature of the entire Church, were "caught up right into the third heaven" and "heard words said that cannot and may not be spoken" (1

Cor 12:2 and 4). And each time it was pure grace, a strictly personal charism. Only the apostle John was both the witness of the life and resurrection of Jesus and the visionary on Patmos of the glorified Christ. But the fundamental problem for our reflection is that of the nature of the link established by Christ at Caesarea Philippi between Peter and "the rock."

## Notes

1. Irenaeus, *Adversus Haereses* III, 3, 1–2.
2. Deusdedit, *Coll. canon*, Prol.
3. Letter of the Council of Arles to Sylvester, Bishop of Rome, Mansi 2, 469.

# 3.

# *Pétros* and *Pétra:* Peter and the Rock

Christ's words in Matthew 16:18, "You are Peter and on this rock I will build my Church,"[1] gave rise to many interpretations in the early Church, interpretations, moreover, which were not mutually exclusive.

For not a few of the Fathers, especially in the East (which is why one speaks of "antiochene exegesis"), though not exclusively so, "rock" (*pétra* in Greek) refers to the faith which Peter (*Pétros* in Greek) confessed when Jesus asked him, "who do you say I am," and Peter responded, "You are the Christ, the Son of the living God" (Mt 16:15–16). The Church is founded upon Christ as the Truth. She therefore exists to the extent that there are people who recognize this truth, who confess Peter's faith. In this sense, each of the faithful individually and all the faithful in communion are the "successors" of Peter. "If we also say to ourselves 'You are the Christ, the Son of the living God,' then we too become Peter," wrote Origen, ". . . for whoever is united to Christ becomes Peter."[2] John Chrysostom (followed by many Antiochenes of renown),[3] has Jesus say, "On this rock (*pétra*) I will build my Church, that is to say, on the faith of your confession."[4] In the West the commentaries of Ambrose and Augustine are similar. "Try to be like rock," says Ambrose. "Search for the rock not without but within yourself. Your rock is your action, your mind . . . it is faith, and faith is the foundation of the Church. If you are like rock, you will be in the Church, because the Church is resting on rock."[5] Augustine says, "The Church is built upon the one whom Peter confessed when he said, 'You are the Christ, the Son of the living God.' That is how Peter came to be called the rock, and he represented the person of the Church who is built upon this rock and who has received the keys of the kingdom of heaven. Indeed, Christ did not say to Peter, 'you are rock (*pétra*)' but 'you are Peter (*Pétrus*)."[6] For the rock (*pétra*) was Christ whom he confessed, as does the whole Church, and he, Simon, received the name of Peter (*Pétrus*).[7]

Communion among the churches is achieved through the eucharist. The Church is not only built on Christ as Truth, but also on Christ as Life, and this Life comes to the faithful through the eucharist and through all the sacraments (including the reading of the gospel), of which the eucharist is the center and the source of radiance. But the sacraments seek the apostolic witness of the episcopacy. Witnesses to God's fidelity in these "mysteries," judges of the Truth which they all preserve, pastors of the flock of Christ, the bishops are as such Peter's successors. In the archetypal Church, the church of Jerusalem between Pentecost and the dispersion of the apostles, Peter certainly presided in the place of Christ at the eucharistic meal, the first to anticipate the episcopal charism. For Cyprian of Carthage, each bishop in his church and all the bishops together, *in solidum*, sit on the Chair of Peter (*Cathedra Petri*). In a celebrated passage from his treatise, *The Unity of the Catholic Church* (and here it does not matter that of the two versions of this text one mentions the primacy of Rome) Cyprian affirms that the words of Jesus in Matthew

16 instituted the entire episcopacy. Through Peter, who speaks in the name of all the disciples, Jesus confers on all the *cathedra*, the episcopal ministry. "He gives to all the apostles an equal power." Roman primacy, mentioned in one of the two versions, finds its place in the context of this episcopal collegiality; by no means does it place the bishop of Rome outside the common episcopacy, which Cyprian understands as a whole, and of which each bishop holds a portion. If, therefore, in each apostle there is Peter, each bishop, by virtue of his apostolic mission, is a successor of Peter.

Augustine speaks similarly in one of his homilies. Peter "is not the only one among the disciples who is worthy of pasturing the Lord's sheep. If Christ speaks only to one, it is to emphasize unity. Indeed, so that you may know that it is the Church who has received the keys to the kingdom of heaven, listen to what the Lord has said elsewhere to all the apostles: 'Receive the Holy Spirit.' And later, 'Anyone whose sins you have forgiven, they are forgiven; anyone whose sins you retain, they are retained' (Jn 20:22–23)."[8]

Gradually, however, especially in the West (with Hilary of Poitiers, Jerome and to a certain extent Ambrose) but also in the East (with Basil),[9] the link between the confession of Peter and his person is emphasized. The rock (*pétra*) is the person of Peter as the one who confesses the apostolic faith. Another link will be established, but not immediately, between Peter confessing and the bishop of Rome bearing witness.

Indeed, by no means immediately. Peter was not the first bishop of Rome (or of Antioch for that matter): one should not confuse the role of apostle, whose unique and untransmissible witness and missionary mobility we have already mentioned, with that of bishop. Historians, in fact,

do not know if there existed in Rome a monarchical episcopacy (exercised by a single individual) before the
mid-second century, as opposed to a college of presbyters or
*episkopoi* (overseers): two words from which we get the terms
"priest" and "bishop" but which originally meant the elders
of a community. It may be that the list of bishops which
Irenaeus produced, and of which Peter was obviously not a
part, provides the names of the most illustrious members of
this college, such as Clement of Rome.

Besides, the priority or primacy of Rome during the early
centuries had nothing to do with the person of its bishop
but with the prestige of the local church within a vast
communion of churches. It is the church of Rome "which
presides in charity," says Ignatius of Antioch in his *Letter to
the Romans*.

When the see was vacant, as happened during the persecution under Decius between January 250 and the spring of
251, it was the college of priests and deacons that spoke in
the name of the church of Rome, sending a number of
letters to Carthage where a serious crisis reigned.

It is only with Callistus (around 220) or perhaps Victor
(192–194) that the bishops of Rome base their primacy on
the words of Jesus in Matthew 16:13–19 and especially on
those in Luke 22:31–32 and John 21:15–18. The first
explicit testimony in Christian thought is that of Tertullian
who, on each occasion, situates Petrine primacy either in the
unity of the episcopacy or in the unity of the people of God:

1. "Would Peter have been ignorant of anything, he who
was called the rock on whom the Church should be built?
. . . *Would something have been hidden from John?*"[10]

2. "Remember that the Lord left the keys to Peter, and
through him to the Church, *keys which each one carries with
him if, when asked, he confesses the faith.*[11]

Thus the idea develops that Peter received from Christ a particular charism that made him the first among the apostles, and that the bishop of Rome is his successor or, rather, his vicar, the one who inherits this charism. The bishop of Rome "succeeded" Peter, but he had to harmonize his testimony with that of Paul. His service was to remember and defend, as well as to spread the faith that Peter and Paul confessed. "The primacy," says Ambrose, "is one of confession, not of honor; of faith, not jurisdiction."[12] The role of Rome, its petrine charism, is therefore to keep watch over the communion of the local churches, to prevent them from breaking away, to intervene at the request of any one of them (as at Corinth in 96 or again around 170), to serve as a point of reference to anyone seeking insertion in one of the most prestigious of the apostolic traditions. In the course of the early centuries, Rome did not lay claim to jurisdiction over the other churches, but she possessed an "authority" (not "power"), a particular faculty of "reception," and exercised an expansive and loving solicitude. The pauline dimension of the see of Rome, to a certain extent prophetic, was fully in play.

Since the fourth century, Roman authority has tended to express itself in specific canonical powers and, depending on the place, in a variety of ways. In a large part of Italy, in those areas called "suburban," that is, situated near Rome, the bishop of Rome had the powers of a metropolitan. In western Europe, his future patriarchate, the bishop of Rome enjoyed furthermore a right of appeal. For Africa and the East, whose churches were organized autonomously, with their own primatial centers and according to a collegial model, Rome served as a court of appeal in case of conflict, since she was the first see in what would come to be called the Pentarchy (Rome, Constantinople, Alexandria,

Antioch, Jerusalem). Until the eighth century, moreover, the election of the bishop of Rome was subject to the approval of the emperor.

By the time of Leo the Great, pope from 440–461, the doctrine of Roman primacy was complete. The bishop of Rome represents the perpetual presence of Peter, prince of the apostles. He is at the helm of the universal Church, "the first among bishops, the head (*princeps*) of the entire Church." This legacy of Peter is conceived along the lines of Roman law: the heir, in taking the place of the deceased, becomes juridically identical with him. It is then but a small step from Rome as "spiritual authority," a place of reference, a "touchstone" as J.-M. Tillard says,[13] to Rome claiming a "power" over all the local churches. But with the Eastern Church remaining close to the traditional conception, we shall see how a balance came to be established. Moreover, Leo himself never intervened except to bear witness to the truth and to insist on respect for the laws of the local churches. He is aware both of the "succession" to Peter by the episcopate—the *forma Petri*, he says, is present in each province—and of the same "succession" by the faithful: "It is in the entire Church that Peter says each day, 'You are the Christ, the Son of the living God.' Every tongue that confesses the Lord like this is quickened by the magisterium of this word."[14] And Leo likes to recall that his role is one of "watchman" or "sentinel."

The ambiguity was momentarily resolved by Gregory I, Gregory the Great, whom the East has nicknamed *Dialogos*, after the title of one of his works in which the mystical theology of Benedict is masterfully expounded. As Battifol observes, for Gregory, the primacy (*principatus*) over the universal Church, which the bishop of Rome inherited from the apostle Peter, gives him a primacy of solicitude, of responsibility and divine assistance. But it would be a significant error to confuse this with the rights which, as metropolitan, he exercises over the bishops of his province. "The *principatus* is an assistance that comes into play when someone appeals to the pope and when the pope deems his intervention opportune and necessary. The *principatus* has nothing to do with organized and imposed centralization."[15]

Gregory protested against the title of "ecumenical patriarch," which the patriarchs of Constantinople had just taken on (in order to affirm their primacy in the context of the "ecumenical" empire). No bishop, declared Gregory, can call himself universal without rendering void the ministry of other bishops. He attached extreme importance to his title of *servus servorum dei*, "servant of the servants of God."

## Notes

1. Alas, the word-play in French between Pierre (Peter) and pierre (rock) is not so conveniently translated into English (Trans.).

2. Origen, *Commentaria in Evangelium secundum Matthaeum*, PG 13, 997–1004.

3. Theodoret of Cyr, Epistula, PG 83, 1249; John Damascene, *Homilia in Transfigurationem Domini*, PG 96, 556.

4. John Chrysostom, *Homilia LIV in Matthaeum*, PG 58, 534.

5. Ambrose, *Traité sur l'Évangile de Luc*, SC 45, trans. G. Tissot (Paris: Cerf, 1956), pp. 264–265.

6. *Pétrus* is the latinized form of the biblical Greek *Pétros*.

7. St Augustine, *Retractationes* I, XXI, 1.

8. Augustine, *Sermo* 295, 2–8.

9. Basil, *Adv. Eunomium* II, 4, PG 20, 580.

10. Tertullian, *De præscriptione* 22, PL 2, 14.

11. Tertullian, *Scorpiace*, 10, PL 2, 142.

12. Ambrose, *De Spiritu Sancto*, PL 16, 826.

13. J.-M. Tillard, *L'éveque de Rome* (Paris, 1982), p. 112.
14. Leo the Great, *Sermo* III, PL 54, 145–146.
15. P. Battifol, *Saint Grégoire le Grand* (Paris, 1928), pp. 188–189.

# 4.

# The Reception of Roman Primacy in the East

Until the beginning of the fifth century, the Fathers in the East commonly applied the gospel texts concerning the petrine ministry only to Peter the apostle and not to the bishop of Rome. That the East never questioned the so-called privileges of the church of Rome is underlined by canon 6 of the first ecumenical council, held at Nicaea in 325, which did not establish but recognized the privileges of Alexandria, Antioch and Rome. These were the three sees whose bishops from the time of the apostles Eusebius lists in his *Ecclesiastical History*, proof of the importance he gave to apostolic origin: "petrine" origin, as Rome will take pleasure in pointing out, for Peter was one of the founders of the church of Antioch, and Mark, who played the same part in Alexandria, was his disciple.

What is more, in the eyes of the Eastern churches the basis of Roman primacy remained for a long time almost entirely dependent on the presence of the tombs of the apostles Peter and Paul and of the "trophies" of their martyrdom in the empire's traditional capital. For them Peter and Paul were still in some sense personally present in Rome. In the fifth century, Theodoret of Cyrrhus wrote to

Pope Leo the Great that Rome was the "metropolis of religion," because it is "the home of the apostles."[1]

The primacy of the bishop of Rome was gradually recognized by the East (within limits, which we will attempt to examine at the end of this chapter and especially in the following chapter, devoted to the relationship between pope and council). An important, while not ecumenical, council at Serdica (343–344) defined, to the benefit of the bishop of Rome and of the universal Church, a law not exactly of appeal but of abrogation: the pope could refuse the evidence of a bishop and send "presbyters from among his entourage" to participate in the appeal judgment rendered by the neighboring bishops of the province where the dispute arose. With time these canons of Serdica were accepted in the East and confirmed by the primarily (but not exclusively) eastern synod of Quinisext (or Trullan synod), which was principally dedicated to questions of discipline and met at Constantinople in 692.

Beginning in the fifth century, the eastern Fathers Flavian, Theodoret of Cyrrhus, Maximus the Confessor, and Theodore the Studite, spoke unambiguously of the pope as the "successor of Peter." It was likewise with Byzantine legislation: whenever the Pentarchy was mentioned in the *Novels* of Justinian, the church of Rome was always at the top of the list, and its bishop referred to as "the first among priests" (the word is used here in the wider sense of episcopate).[2]

The fourth ecumenical council, gathered at Chalcedon in 451, wrote in its message to Leo the Great: "You came to us; you have been for everyone the interpreter of the voice of the blessed Peter. . . . We were some 520 bishops whom you guided, as the head guides the members." The Fathers of the sixth ecumenical council (Constantinople, 680–681) wrote similarly to Pope Agathon: "We place ourselves in your hands, you who occupy the first see of the universal Church, you who rest on the firm rock of faith."

The decree of union (*Hénotikon*) with the monophysites, promulgated at the end of the fifth century by Emperor Zenon, incurred the protest of Rome and resulted in a schism of thirty-five years between East and West. Under Justin I, imperial policy turned away from any christological compromise, and reconciliation with Rome was achieved. It was then that Pope Hormisdas asked and obtained in 519 the signature of Patriarch John of Constantinople to the following formula: "The first condition of our salvation is to guard the orthodox rule of faith and not to depart from any of the decrees of the Fathers. One cannot overlook the words of Our Lord Jesus Christ who says: 'You are Peter and on this rock I shall build my Church.' This affirmation is borne out in deeds, for the catholic[3] religion has always been preserved without blemish in the Apostolic See. We hope to be worthy of living in unity in this communion, which the Apostolic See preaches and in which resides, whole and true, the firm foundation of the Christian religion." The text concludes with the verification of the "catholic communion" by "agreement with the Apostolic See."[4] This declaration was signed by the majority of the eastern bishops.

In the East, therefore, one turned to Rome when the faith was in danger and the harmony of the Pentarchy threatened. The attitude of Maximus the Confessor demonstrates both the depth of the trust and, subsequently, the extreme reserve found necessary when the pope seemed no longer to mirror the faith of Peter, when *Pétros* and *pétra* went their separate ways, however slightly. During the monothelite controversy, which we have already mentioned, Maximus, a simple monk but an immense theologian of universal renown, gained the support of Rome. At his behest, the pope convoked the Lateran Council in 649, which affirmed the full human freedom of Christ and which, for Maximus, had the weight of an ecumenical council (called by the pope, it should be noted, and not by the emperor). In the midst of this controversy, and when the support of Rome became clear, Maximus affirmed that Rome was "the head and metropolis of the churches," "the 'rock' truly solid and unmoving . . . the greatest apostolic church."[5] The church of Rome, he said, "has the keys of the faith and of the orthodox confession."[6] These texts were confirmed by the martyrdom of Pope Martin I, who was taken from Rome by Byzantine troops, judged and condemned at Constantinople, and who died of his maltreatment on the road into exile. A friend of Maximus, Theodore Spudaeus, denounced "the persecution leveled against our holy Father, now in blessedness with God, faithful prince of the apostles and universal apostolic pope, and at the same time against the catholic Church."[7] With great profundity Theodore showed that the pope had truly become the successor of Peter, chief of the apostles, in suffering martyrdom, "offering himself in sacrifice, while imitating and following Christ to the end," as also the apostle Peter did.[8]

But whenever Rome seemed to waver, ready to compromise, were it only by silence, the example of Maximus recalled that the pope's confession of faith could never take the place of a personal act of faith. The petrine charism cannot replace personal conscience, humble and courageous, based on the internal evidence of the Good News. "Yesterday, the eighteenth of the month (April 658), on the day of mid-Pentecost,[9] the patriarch [the new Pope Vitalian had just taken up again with Constantinople] spoke to me as follows: 'To what church do you belong? To the church of Constantinople? to Rome? to Antioch? to Alexandria? to Jerusalem? But they are all one. If, then, you belong to the catholic Church, remain at one with it lest in taking a path other than the way of life you meet with something unforeseen.' I said to him: 'The catholic Church is the forthright and saving confession of faith in the God of the universe, who showed this in proclaiming Peter blessed for confessing it forthrightly.' "[10]

Thus it is Peter's "forthright confession" of faith that alone has the power to make him the "rock" on which Christ founded his Church. Private conscience, informed by ecclesial communion, must, if need be, rise up in opposition, but its path should be that of martyrdom, not rebellion. This is Paul, once again, "opposing [Peter] to his face, since he is manifestly in the wrong." It is a regrettable fact that the importance of Paul in defining the primacy of Rome diminished little by little until, in the sixteenth century, seeking to stem the tide of the Reformation which claimed the authority of the charismatic apostle, Rome denounced as heretical all those who stressed the equality of Peter and Paul.

Another crisis, which opposed Rome and Constantinople in the ninth century, brought out the fact that for the East, the authority of Rome was certainly founded upon the words of Christ to Peter but also on the brotherhood of the bishops and respect for the canons. "A primacy of duties rather than of rights."[11]

The election of Photius as Patriarch of Constantinople had given rise to controversy (as a layman, he had had to pass through all the degrees of priesthood in a matter of days). But in May 859, the great majority of bishops confirmed his election, and the turmoil was subsiding when

Pope Nicholas I intervened. His legates, sent to investigate, demanded that the condemnation of Photius's rival, Ignatius, be reviewed by a council in their presence. The Byzantines accepted this, both out of respect for Rome and because proceedings conformed to the canons of Serdica. The council thus convened in 861 confirmed the condemnation of Ignatius and the election of Photius.

The more extreme supporters of Ignatius—a group of monks opposed to the humanism of Photius—renewed their appeal to Rome, and Nicholas I deposed Photius in April 863 and returned the possession of the patriarchate to Ignatius. Since the canons gave Rome only a right of abrogation, it was an extraordinary decision. Standing confidently on this traditional right, Photius and the majority of Greek bishops challenged the decisions of Rome.

The crisis was heightened when doubt emerged over the correctness of the Roman faith: Latin missionaries at work in Bulgaria were teaching the creed with the addition of *filioque* (unknown to the East).[12] The Council of Constantinople (867) deposed and condemned the pope partly because of this addition, made without ecumenical agreement, and partly for having attempted to transform his primacy into an immediate jurisdiction over all the churches, contrary to tradition and the declarations of the councils.

Under Hadrian II, who succeeded Nicholas I, Rome profited from a political upheaval in Byzantium: Emperor Michael III was assassinated by Basil the Macedonian, who took possession of the crown. Photius took issue with the murderer, who banished him to a monastery. A council held at Constantinople in 869–870, under the combined pressure of the legates and the emperor, contented itself with ratifying the decisions of the pope who, under his own

authority, annulled the conciliar decrees of 867 and anathematized Photius. The majority of the Byzantine bishops
did not take part in the new synod, which once again
condemned Photius and restored Ignatius. After a time
Ignatius, bowing to the wish of the episcopate, was recon-
ciled with Photius who, after his rival's death, ascended
once again to the patriarchal throne.

The new pope, John VIII (872–882), wanted to restore
the unity of the Church by a return to tradition. A genuine
council of union—the only one to date which has been
crowned with success—gathered at Hagia Sophia in
879–880[13] in the presence of the papal legates and the
eastern patriarchs, a council that truly represented the
Pentarchy. The synod of 869–870 was annulled; Photius
was solemnly reinstated; the Nicene-Constantinopolitan
Creed was proclaimed without the addition of *filioque*.
Finally, the council recalled the legitimacy of local customs
in all their diversity. As for Roman primacy, it is not clear
that it was understood by the eastern bishops in legal or
juridical terms, but rather within a framework of collegiality.

This leads us to consider the dialectic of papacy and
ecumenical council during the first millennium.

## Notes

1. W. de Vries, *Orient et Occident, les structures ecclésiales vues dans
l'histoire des sept premiers conciles œcuméniques* (Paris, 1974), pp. 138–139.
2. Novel128, cap. 3.
3. At this time the words "catholic" and "orthodox" had no sectarian
meaning. In both East and West the faith was spoken of as "orthodox"
and the church as "catholic." Whence the absurdity of a certain "uniate"
language, orthodox as well as catholic, which maintains that Gaul (i.e.,

France) was then "orthodox" and Greece "catholic" in the confessional sense of these words.

4. Denzinger, 363–365.

5. Mansi 10, 677 A–678 B.

6. Maximus the Confessor, *Opuscula theologica et polemica*, PG 91, 137 C.

7. Mansi 10, 857 B.

8. R. Devreesse, "Le texte grec de l'Hypomnaticum de Théodore Spoudée," *Analecta Bollandiana* 58 (1935) 79.

9. A feast celebrated in the Byzantine rite on the Wednesday of the fourth week after Easter and commenting on the words of Christ, "Let him who thirsts come to me and drink."

10. Maximus the Confessor, *Ad Anastasium monachum*, PG 90, 132 A.

11. J. Meijer, *A Successful Council of Union*, p. 133, cited in Alexis van Bunnen, "Le Concile de Constantinople de 879–880," *Contacts*, no. 117, 1 (1982) 53.

12. The second ecumenical council (Constantinople, 381) stated clearly the divinity of the Holy Spirit "who proceeds from the Father" (Jn 15:26). The West, in the course of its own reflection, especially through Ambrose and Augustine, added "and from the Son" (in Latin *filioque*), a formula which has never been calmly examined by an ecumenical council.

13. One of the greatest Orthodox theologians and historians of our time, Father John Meyendorff, wished that this council of 879–880, with its successful union, might come to figure as the eighth council on the Catholic lists of ecumenical councils (the Orthodox list stops at the seventh) instead of, as is still the case today, the synod of disunion of 869–870, which was annulled two years later with full papal agreement.

# 5.

# The Pope and the Ecumenical Council in the Undivided Church

## The Protagonists: Two Plenitudes in Opposition

## The Pope

At the Council of Ephesus (431) the representative of Pope Celestine reminded those present that Christ established Peter as the foundation of the Church. Since Peter continued to be present in his successors to exercise through them the role of arbiter, Celestine, in sending legates to the Council, did so precisely as successor and vicar of Peter.[1] In his letter of 15 March 432 to the council,[2] he based himself on the solicitude he was bound to have for the entire Church, itself an expression of the solicitude of Peter, which extends to all people. He cited 2 Corinthians 11:29 on concern for all the churches, a text which subsequent popes would never tire of quoting.

At the time of Chalcedon (453), Pope Leo the Great declared that the Lord had conferred their powers on the apostles through the intermediary of Peter,[3] an idea which would continue to play a role in how Rome understood the

At the sixth ecumenical council (Constantinople III), the Fathers, restoring the unity of the Church, anathematized not only the patriarchs of Constantinople, Alexandria and Antioch, but also Pope Honorius: all dead by then, and all compromised in the monothelite controversy.

At the same council, the letter of Pope Agathon, his *suggestio* (*anaphora*) was respectfully introduced for debate, scrutinized, and only at the end received fully, because it was in accordance—communion in time—with the decisions of Chalcedon and the entire tradition: the gospels, apostles, councils. . . . It is therefore communion in space and above all in time which verifies the truth.

Likewise at Nicaea II, Tarasius, the new Patriarch of Constantinople, in his first letter to Pope Hadrian, insisted that the true president of the council was Christ, present in the gospels, which had been placed in the midst of the assembly. Certainly the letter of the pope was read out, but so were the letters of the eastern patriarchs and the testimonies of the Fathers—always the reference to communion both in space and in time.

## Notes

1. ACO I/I 3, 60.
2. ACO I 7, 145.
3. Leo the Great, *Sermo* 4, 2, PL 54, 149.
4. Mansi, 11, 234, 235, 239, 242.
5. Mansi 12, 1086.
6. ACO II/I 2, 126.
7. The name given to the extracts or works of Theodore of Mopsuestia, Ibas of Edessa and Theodoret of Cyr, who were accused, like Nestorius, of compromising the unity of divine and human natures in Christ.
8. ACO II/I 2, 130.
9. ACO, IV 1, 209.

# 6.

# The Pope and the Ecumenical Council in the Undivided Church

## Miracles and Compromise of "Communion"

This period was marked both in East and West by a very strong sense of ecclesial communion. Communion is the bond that unites the faithful among themselves to form a single Church, *fidelium universitas*, says Leo, and the ground and determinant of this communion is the true faith. Unity of faith is acknowledged and expressed in the reciprocal granting and receiving of communion.

## The Pope in Communion with the Council

As we have seen, Rome took the view that its judgment was of itself decisive and that the council must ratify it. Nevertheless the popes were far from rejecting outright the collegial principle of the Church. It was the faith of Peter, the faith of all, which they meant to defend. Besides, every decision of Rome was itself collegial, emanating not from an individual but from the Roman synod.

In his letter to the Council of Ephesus, Pope Celestine expressed his desire that the assembly might come around to his decision, but only, he made clear, if this decision was seen to serve the common good, "a measure ensuring the peace of the entire Church."[1] The pope saw the council as the assembly of the apostles's successors assisted by the Holy Spirit. "The assembly of bishops," he wrote, "bears witness to the presence of the Holy Spirit." The apostolic Council of Jerusalem lived again in the "holy college of bishops." It was to the pope and the bishops collectively that the Lord entrusted the common responsibility to teach the nations. "The Holy Spirit has established the bishops 'to pasture God's Church' (Acts 20:28)."[2]

After the closing of the council, Celestine wrote to the clergy and people of Constantinople that "Nestorius has been reproved both by the universal Church and by our own pronouncement." At the council "the Holy Spirit, ever living in his priests, decreed what was in the best interests of all."

Now let us consider the case of Chalcedon. Pope Leo considered null and void the hijacking of Ephesus in 449, but he was aware that he could not annul this council on his own authority. This is why he proposed that the emperor convoke a new council (which he would have liked to have seen held in Italy, but failed to achieve). It is clear that Leo, despite his trenchant assertions, was not an autocrat. He took his decisions in agreement with the Roman synod. In his letter of confirmation of Chalcedon he called the members of the Council "his brothers and co-bishops."[3] He always sought a consensus from the college of bishops and from the universal Church. His representatives certainly affirmed that the church of Rome "is the head of all the churches"[4] and its bishop the "archbishop of all the churches"—in Latin: "Pope of the universal Church."[5] But this title is easily misunderstood, for Leo never claimed the right to govern as bishop each of the individual churches. Rather he understood his authority as bearing an essential witness to the truth, which, as he himself said, did not belong to him: it was the faith of the Church as the apostle Peter first proclaimed it.[6] That is why he was pleased that his "Tome" was acknowledged by the council, "confirmed," he wrote, "by the undisputed accord of the entire assembly of brethren."[7] Two conceptions, verbally at odds, had come together in the truth that embodies accord at a higher level, an accord that is not juridical and cannot be objectified.

Leo worked very hard to ensure that Chalcedon was received by everyone, for conciliar authority, he said, was founded on the assistance of the Holy Spirit.

At Constantinople II, Pope Vigilius, having arrived in the capital, refused either to take part in the council or to join in the condemnation of certain texts that he considered orthodox, whereupon the council declared that he was excluded from the catholic communion, and his name was erased from the records. But six months after the end of the council, Vigilius recognized it, and his successors did likewise. So it was that the popes and the entire Church, both in the West and in the East, acknowledged the ecumenical legitimacy of a council that excommunicated a pope because he had opposed it. This council had refused to recognize the pope's right to make valid decisions on his own in matters of faith. It would seem that Vigilius's successors were in no way scandalized by this, for they vigorously enforced the fifth ecumenical council. Gregory the Great, in particular, threatened to anathematize anyone who refused to accept the condemnations of this council. Councils, he said, express the unanimity of the Church.

In 649 under Martin I, the Lateran Council reaffirmed all the theological formulas of Constantinople II and specified that the five ecumenical councils had to be acknowledged down to the last detail: which will have included the excommunication of Vigilius.

The sixth ecumenical council, with the agreement of Rome, condemned Pope Honorius as a heretic (he had taken a more than dubious position on the monothelite controversy), and this condemnation was reaffirmed in the profession of faith pronounced by each bishop of Rome after his election—at least until the eleventh-century Gregorian reforms.

## The East in Communion with Rome

The council "received" in freedom, but also with appropriate attention and respect, the judgments of Rome. A document prepared in advance by the pope would often play a very important role in the common reflection and often find itself inserted, though not without modifications, in the decrees of the council.

At Ephesus in 431, the Fathers declared at the beginning of their definition: "Constrained by the canons and by the letter of our holy father and co-minister Celestine. . ."[8] Constrained not juridically but by prestige, as it were. Later the council became more specific: "We have praised the very holy and beloved of God Celestine, bishop of Rome, who had condemned even before our pronouncement the heretical positions of Nestorius and anticipated us in the judgment to be levelled against him."[9] After reading Celestine's letter, the Council acclaimed "the new Peter, Celestine, and the new Paul, Cyril." Whereupon there burst forth the charismatic acclamations: "Celestine is one with the council! One Celestine, one Cyril and the faith of the *oikoumene*!"[10]

During the backwash of the Council of Ephesus, the reconciliation (pressed for by the emperor) between Antioch and Alexandria in 433 and the "hijacking" of 449, the appeals made to Rome by the East increased. On 31 July 432, John of Antioch wrote to Pope Sixtus II that he was seated on the apostolic throne and was a beacon for the entire Church of Christ.[11] Two eastern bishops who refused the somewhat forced reconciliation of 433, Euthyrius of Thyne and Helladius of Tarsus, addressed themselves to the pope as to "someone who has been designated by God to take the helm."[12] Theodoret of Cyrrhus, let us not forget, also requested Rome's judgment, as did Flavian, the new archbishop of Constantinople.

At Chalcedon the tension between the monarchical principle and the conciliar principle in the government of the Church became more explicit—its mode of resolution, too. The East emphasized conciliarity without, however, denying papal primacy, but without conceiving it along the same lines as Leo the Great. Rome strongly affirmed her primacy but could not impose her claim to define truth on her own, or set herself up as the sole criterion of communion. The bishops's awareness of collegial authority was too strong. Not that this inhibited the charismatic acclamations that followed the reception of the "Tome" of Leo: "Peter has spoken through the mouth of Leo."[13]

The affair of canon 28 of Chalcedon is a prime example. This canon established the primatial pecking order—whereby Constantinople came after Rome—according to what was known as the "political principle," that is to say, the importance of the respective capitals. In the background, moreover, the properly religious meaning given to the "city" as center of the world and anticipation of the eschatological city can be discerned; but whether pagan or

Hebrew, the meaning certainly was not Christian, for it held no awareness of the distinction between the kingdom of God and that of Caesar.

At Chalcedon, therefore, this canon was confirmed despite the protests of the Roman legates, who insisted on the petrine charism of the bishop of Rome as opposed to the "urban" (and imperial) one. Then, as the council was about to end, Archbishop Anatolius of Constantinople, the Council Fathers, and the emperor himself strove to obtain Leo's recognition of canon 28. In the council's letter, the primacy of the pope was clearly acknowledged. Not only had Leo been "the interpreter of the voice of Peter," but, in order to justify the promotion of Constantinople, the council asked that a ray of the light of Rome's apostolicity shine on the "other Rome," which thus would become spiritually one with the first.[14] In the face of Leo's persistent refusal, Anatolius, in a letter addressed to Leo, virtually withdrew canon 28, blaming its adoption on the clergy of Constantinople.[15]

At the sixth ecumenical council, the letter of Pope Agathon was received with the same enthusiasm with which Chalcedon had received the "Tome" of Leo. "Peter has spoken through Agathon!" And the council asked the pope to ratify its decisions (the verb used was *kanonizein*), which was what Pope Leo II did as Agathon's successor.

One can discern two tendencies among the Fathers of this council, but it would be a mistake to over-systematize them with the juridical mindset that will later come to characterize the West. It is more a question of shifting sensitivities with frequent boundary-crossing. On the one hand there were those (seemingly more numerous) who said, "Peter has spoken through Agathon," because his letter expressed the faith of Peter. They recognized Rome as the first see, whose *auctoritas*, that is, prestige and moral authority, was beyond question. For the others Rome possessed, by the will of God, a real petrine ministry with a certain primacy of jurisdiction. Therefore Peter spoke in a privileged way through Agathon, because Agathon was his successor and vicar.

The first group, however, would not have said that Peter spoke through the mouth of just *any* bishop. They said it of the bishop of *Rome*. Equally, the second group did not think the petrine ministry of the pope could function of itself; it worked in communion with the council, in communion with and at the service of the Church.

These two tendencies were again in evidence before and during the seventh ecumenical council, but the latter was now dominant: the ecclesiastical institution in Byzantium, as well as the emperors, had taken the side of the iconoclasts, and the defenders of icons had found no support other than that of Rome, to whom they turned on the basis of her "solicitude for all the churches." When Empress Irene approached Pope Hadrian about re-establishing the legitimacy and veneration of images, she was forced to admit that her predecessors and the bishops of her Church had been in error. Here for the first time one can see a new strand appear in Byzantine thought, namely the theme of a mysterious division *within* the Church: Constantinople and the entire patriarchate, while not actually and categorically outside the Church, needed to be reintegrated. It was up to the pope and the council to bring this about. The pope, wrote Irene, has the "principal priesthood," which traces its origin to Christ. He is "the most holy head," who "presides from the see of Peter." Let him come himself or send his representatives to take part in the council, which will put an end to the division in the Church, whose head is Christ himself, our true God."[16]

During the council the pope's representatives enjoyed immense prestige; they were listed at the beginning of the Acts of the council, with the church of Rome being designated the church of the apostle Peter, and in the name of the pope they were the first to sign the dogmatic declaration of the council.

With regard to this declaration—especially during its difficult gestation—many turned openly to the petrine authority of the pope. This was particularly true of the monks who were fighting against iconoclasm. Tarasius, the new patriarch, a supporter of icons and whose authority was still precarious, had attempted to correspond with the eastern patriarchs but never succeeded. It was certain monks, "pious men" of those patriarchates, who responded to him. When need dictated, they said, a council could be held in the absence of their patriarchs, on condition that, as was the case at the sixth ecumenical council, "the most holy and apostolic pope of Rome gave his approval and were present through his representatives."[17]

In the Acts of the Council, after all the amendments and hence in the definitive text approved by all the Byzantines, can again be found the passage where the pope exhorts the emperors to honor the "vicar of Peter,"[18] and where Rome is called "the head of all the churches of God."

## Notes

1. ACO I/II, 24.
2. Ibid., 22–24.
3. Leo the Great, Epistula 69, PL 54, 892.
4. ACO II/I, 65.
5. ACO II/I, 2, 93.
6. Leo the Great, Epistula 69, PL 54, 892

7. Leo the Great, Epistula 120, PL 54, 1046–1047.

8. ACO I/I, 2, 54.

9. ACO I/I, 3,5.

10. ACO I/I, 3, 5–6. Nestorius refused Mary the title, "Mother of God." Cyril of Alexandria vigorously opposed him.

11. ACO I/I, 7, 158.

12. ACO IV, 145–148.

13. ACO II/I 2, 81.

14. Leo the Great, Epistula 98, PL 54, 952, 958.

15. Leo the Great, Epistula 132, PL 54, 1082–1084.

16. Mansi 12, 984–986.

17. Mansi 12, 1134.

18. Mansi 12, 1058.

# 7.

# A Creative Tension

From the fourth to the ninth centuries, pope and council never ceased to reinforce each other; like waves meeting and mingling, they clashed, yet, transcending the structures, they always ended by collaborating. As Father Yves Congar points out in his introduction to Wilhelm de Vries's book, *Orient et Occident*, the emperor had the authority to convoke a council. He gave its decrees the force of law but, by and large, except in the period of iconoclasm, he did not claim to have the competence to determine doctrine, and the defeat of iconoclasm was the defeat of an attempt at caesaropapism. The pope could hear an appeal, function as a court of annulment, but the canons protected the autonomy of local churches. Councils, almost always with papal accord, clarified doctrine and established the foundations of Church discipline. Nevertheless, as far as truth is concerned, it asserted itself of itself, transcending the contradictions of ecclesial procedures, imposing the confession of the apostolic faith, the faith of Peter.

Widening the focus, one could say that the Church had several aerials for receiving what the Spirit had to say to her:

—The council as an expression of universal communion.

—The pope as being charged with care for this communion and watching over the petrine and pauline correctness of the faith.

—But also the *utilitas* of the people of God, its "sense of the Church," which can express itself in times of major crisis through the witness, the martyrdom, of a lone prophet. "Anyone who is not with me is not with the truth," exclaimed Maximus the Confessor when nearly everyone was content either to keep quiet or to compromise. And Theodore the Studite, witness of orthodoxy during the second outbreak of iconoclasm and persecuted by the majority of bishops and the patriarch himself, affirmed most evangelically that "three believers who were united in the orthodox faith constitute the Church."[1]

The East did not experience primacy in the form that it was to take in the West after the Gregorian reform and the Council of Trent. It refused it in anticipation. But at the time of the ecumenical councils it acknowledged a true Roman primacy and the petrine charism which that presupposes. And this was by no means a simple "primacy of honor," a *primus inter pares*, in the purely honorific sense of these expressions.

What did it entail? It is difficult to say exactly; any precise, juridical definition of the modern type seems out of keeping. On either side theories were evolving which seemed in disaccord; in fact, ecclesial practice ended by transcending them. The pope would write to the council with the intention of imposing an authoritative solution to some problem; his letter was received and listened to with the utmost respect, but *freely* and in the context of *free reflection*. The faith of Peter, indeed, but could it be separated from the vicariate of Peter, if God wanted this latter and the charism that goes with it? But did he want it? The East, at the time of the ecumenical councils, said yes, but differently—differently, that is, from Catholic theologians who in modern times have hardened the texts of a Leo the Great, making them more authoritarian. Certainly, that risk was there already; an evolution could be discerned. Nevertheless Leo never ceased affirming that the purpose of Roman primacy was to serve ecclesial communion, *fidelium universitas*, itself founded upon the "unity of the catholic faith."[2] Moreover, he says time and again that he cannot exercise his charism except in communion with his "brothers and co-bishops"[3] whose rights he respects and safeguards.

It is, in the end, an admirable complementarity, a providential collaboration between popes and councils. The councils only achieved their full ecumenicity through the fruitful contribution of the Roman tomes, however freely debated and amended, through which both the West and the petrine charism expressed themselves. If the councils had not been complemented in this way, the rule of faith by which we live could not have been worked out. Without the popes, more distanced from the political center of the empire and hence more independent (in which particular they joined hands with the monks), the ultimate transcendence of the Church could not have been preserved.

Each of the two structures, taken alone, can be seen to have failed. Under Celestine the papacy vacillated, under Honorius and Vitalian it bent before the wind. From the eighth century on, militarily abandoned by Byzantium, rescued from the Lombards by the Carolingians, it fell back on the West, hardening its pretensions to the point of creating another emperor. In this, too, the tension inherent in the Byzantine "symphony"[4] was replaced by logic of another kind: the absorption by the "spiritual" of the "temporal." Thus was the ground prepared for the schism between West and East.

For its part, the council could not prevent the tearing asunder of the Church in the ancient Christian lands of

Egypt and Syria in the fifth and sixth centuries. Clearly the dogma of Chalcedon was an immense accomplishment; even today it is pushing back the horizons of Christian thought. But how can one forget all those bishops in the Middle East who claimed that the new definition ran counter to Tradition? Philoxenus of Mabbug, for example, who was no heedless theologian of little consequence, disputed the claim that the council had been "received" by the entire Church, a reception which alone, for him, would have obliged acceptance of its decisions. Who was right, one might naïvely ask? Choices are often influenced by geographical, social, cultural, even ethnic factors, but at this time in the East choices were also made according to conscience, as they would be in the West at the time of the pre-Reformation and Reformation, as Maximus the Confessor had made his at the decisive moment. Conscience protects and justifies itself first through polemic. Burrowing deeper over time, it seeks communion, so that it is today that Chalcedon (and Ephesus) can be universally received; it is today, too, that ways can be found of bridging the schism between Orthodox East and Catholic and Protestant West: not through compromise, but through a clearer discovery in the Holy Spirit of the original core of the message.

These schisms aside, the true greatness of the period of the ecumenical councils is precisely that the power of decision rested with no one: neither pope, nor council, nor emperor, nor public feeling. All thought they had the final word, which meant that no one had it except, rightly, the Holy Spirit.

This greatness was more lived out than conceptualized. Roman primacy defined itself in terms of a legalistic logic where tensions were crushed out of existence by a forcible slotting together of structures: the faithful were locked into the power of the episcopate and the latter into the *plenitudo potestatis* of the pope, the prophet was subordinated to the priest, Paul to Peter, perhaps even the Holy Spirit to Christ, as would be achieved in the mediaeval *filioque* quibbles. In the East, the persistence and recurrence of schism was ensured on the one hand, from without, by force of historical circumstance, i.e., the dominance of Islam; on the other, from within, by the mental petrifaction imposed by closed systems, which confer on details a quasi-magical value.

It is our task today, going beyond the words—words which "stick out their tongues at each other," as Antoine de Saint-Exupéry said in *Citadelle*—to reflect on the lived ecclesial experience of a period when, through compromise and miracles, tensions were resolved throughout the greater part of Christendom neither through forcible insertion, nor through violent schism, but after another fashion: and that was surely the free communion of personal consciences in the Holy Spirit.

## Notes

1. Theodore the Studite, Epistulae, PG 99, 1049 B.
2. Leo the Great, Epistula 28, PL 54, 757; *Sermo* 89, PL 54, 446.
3. Leo the Great, Epistula 114, PL 54, 852.
4. The "symphony" describes an ideal of tensions and agreements between the Church and the empire, without one dominating the other.

# 8.

# Some Observations on the Evolution of the Papacy to Vatican I

Little by little, constrained alike by historical events and the logic of a juridical mindset deprived of the counterbalance of the East (the estrangement of the two halves of Christendom having deepened between the eleventh and the fourteenth centuries), Roman primacy showed signs of becoming contaminated by the problem of power: imperial power, to be precise, which, since the crowning of Charlemagne, had been seen as subordinate to pontifical power. This claim rested on an impressive number of faked documents, the "Donation of Constantine" and the decretals, of which the papacy made a quite innocent use. Already, in the works of Leo and in its liturgical celebration of the apostles Peter and Paul, apostolic Rome appeared to have taken over from ancient imperial Rome. Was not the bishop of Rome now *pontifex maximus* just as the emperor had been?

In the middle of the eighth century, as we saw, the popes, threatened by the Lombards and let down by the military weakness of Constantinople, turned to the Franks and formed an alliance with Pepin the Short. The Byzantine holdings in central Italy then became the Papal States (an unheard-of innovation), concern for which would play a large role in papal politics until their annexation by Italy in 1870. The crowning of Charlemagne gave the pope authority over temporal power. Two centuries of stagnation and decadence followed (the depositions of popes, legitimate or not, multiplied during the tenth century), but the following century saw a recovery, thanks to the support of the great monastic reform movement which sprang up in northwestern Europe, a Europe much more alien to the Byzantine world than Italy. The papacy undertook an energetic program to disengage itself from the secular powers— specifically the German emperor and the Roman barons. While a necessary action, it was achieved by pitting power against power: Gregory VII (whence the name Gregorian reform) fostered the popular uprising in Milan and deposed Emperor Henry IV. This was a revolutionary change undreamed of in the East, which would be slow to discover its possibilities.

In this context the *Dictatus papæ* of Gregory VII stood out. The Roman pontiff could depose bishops or transfer a bishop from one see to another (in fact this would not happen until the end of the Middle Ages—and even then not everywhere—and indeed for some countries not until after the secularization brought about by the Revolution and the French Empire). "He can, when he so wishes, ordain clergy in any church." "His decision cannot be modified by anyone, but, alone, he can change the decision of all." Along with this came the claim of power over society as a whole: "Only [the pope] can use the imperial insignia." "The pope is the only person whose feet must be kissed by every prince." "The pope has authority to depose emperors."

It was the first step toward an absolute and centralized monarchy. The pope became the sole legislator in the

Church. He asserted himself over the council, whose decrees were attributed to him. It was a movement from *primatus* to *papatus*, from primacy to papacy. At the beginning of the thirteenth century. Innocent III formulated the teaching that the pope was no longer "vicar of Peter" but *"vicar of Christ."* "Although the successors of the prince of the apostles, we are not however his vicars, nor those of any other apostle or human being, but the vicars of Jesus Christ himself." "The supreme pontiff is not called the vicar of a mere man, but truly the vicar of the true God."[1] This set off rumblings of revolt among the nascent nation states and the movements preaching a return to the gospel. When Boniface VIII proclaimed in November of 1302, in the bull *Unam Sanctam:* "I am pope and emperor," a strange echo of the words of the iconoclastic emperor Leo III, "I am emperor and priest," he brought down on himself the mail gauntlet of William of Nogaret, envoy of Philip the Fair, King of France, and, as rumor had it, a secret Cathar, which only goes to prove that there are many ways of reading history.

The great western schism, which saw first two, then three popes confronting one another, led to a powerful "conciliarist" movement as a reaction. The Council of Constance, on 6 April 1415, voted the decree *Haec Sancta Synodus.* The council "holds directly from Christ the power to which all owe obedience, irrespective of their state or dignity—were it papal—regarding what pertains to the faith, to the eradication of schism, and the general reform of the Church both in its head and in its members."

This "moderate conciliarism" was soon overtaken by the "radical conciliarism" of the Council of Basel (1431–1449), which saw the pope merely as the agent who implemented the decisions of the council. The adoption of this extreme position put the movement beyond the pale for a few decades. Once again, the possibility of creative tension between pope and council was overlooked, as one or other claimed the dominance. If it was no longer the pope, it was the council; the problem, essentially juridical, remained the same.

At exactly the same time a twofold error led to the failure of the council of union held at Florence (1438–1439). (The Byzantine emperor thought the pope was still the theocratic sovereign of the West, while the pope imagined that this emperor was the absolute head of the Church in the East.)

It was a great philosopher, Nicholas of Cusa, friend of the humanist theologians of Byzantium, who (vainly) took it upon himself to recall to the heart of Western Christendom the authentic tradition of the Church. He refused to decide who, whether pope or council, should be superior to the other. The ideal to be pursued was agreement between the two. In case of disagreement, the important thing was to know "on which side lay the support of the universal Church." "It is not a relationship of authority or submission, either in one direction or the other, valid in all circumstances." Only the Church could attest to the ecclesiality of pope or council.[2]

Nothing, finally, could prevent the crisis of the Reformation, with its radical critique of a papal infallibility which appeared self-determining, and the consequent deep and still unhealed division in Western Christendom. Paul separated from Peter, and the *plenitudo potestatis* of the pope, far from ensuring the unity of the Church, compromised it.

After this amputation, effected with fire and sword, the Counter Reformation allowed the papacy to secure its positions. In the wake of the Council of Trent, Robert

Bellarmine could write: "The Supreme Pontiff is the vicar of Christ and he represents Christ for us as he was when he lived among humankind."[3] And again, "the Church is the society of all the faithful, united in the confession of the same faith, in participating in the same sacraments, under the authority of legitimate pastors and above all under that of the sole vicar of Christ on earth, the Roman Pontiff."[4] The Church was beginning to look like a universal state, with the pope as its head, who appointed the bishops, approved concordats with heads of state, with the help no longer of legates but of permanent nuncios, diplomats at the service of a centralized administration. At the same time, the myth of the center, a mental construct found in most religions but which apostolic Christianity had exploded into the omnipresence of the Word and of the eucharist,[5] passed from Jerusalem to Rome, as the career of Ignatius of Loyola attests.

The gradual secularization of nation states since the Enlightenment and the French Revolution completed the process of returning local churches to papal jurisdiction. When the Papal States collapsed (to be restored, symbolically, only in 1929), the papacy, together with a large number of Catholics, horrified by the countless attacks made on them by a hostile modern world against which they wished to raise an impregnable rampart, elicited the definitions of the First Vatican Council (1870). On the one hand there was the dogma of the infallibility, *ex sese non ex consensu* (of themselves and not by consensus), of definitions concerning faith and morals that were promulgated by the pope *ex cathedra*; besides this, the council affirmed his "immediate" and "truly episcopal" jurisdiction over the entire Church: "If anyone says that the Roman Pontiff is only charged with inspection or direction and not with the full and supreme power of jurisdiction over the entire Church . . . or that he has only a very important part of this supreme power and not its complete fullness; or that his power is not ordinary or immediate over each and every church as well as over each and every pastor and member of the flock, let him be anathema."[6]

Although the Council Fathers stressed that they did not wish to part from the traditional faith so clearly expressed by the great councils, "where East met West in a union of faith and love,"[7] the dogma of Vatican I has struck the Orthodox (as well as other non-Catholic Christians) as unacceptable. An Orthodox will even wonder if the authentic ecclesial conscience of the Latin Church (and its Greek Catholic extensions) was not expressed in the perfectly clear statements of the (unheard) minority. Archbishop Spalding of Baltimore quoted Gregory the Great: "My honor . . . is the firm strength of my brothers in the episcopal state."[8] Bishop de Las Cases of Hippo feared that "in effect the pope remains the only true bishop in the entire Church, the others being certainly bishops in name but, in reality, mere vicars."[9] Bishop Bravard of Coutances expressed and clarified the same fear: ". . . the bishops appear to be no more than the vicars of the Roman Pontiff, removable at his behest, whereas Christ chose twelve whom he called his apostles, and all of us, who are appointed to a see, believe that when we received the fullness of the priesthood, we were wedded to that see, truly and irrevocably before God, and that we were bound to it as to a spouse."[10] The courageous Greek Catholic Patriarch of Antioch, Gregory II Youssef, proclaimed that the Church "was not an absolute monarchy." After he expressed his view to Pius IX that the definitions prepared were not in accordance with Tradition, there came the famous reply: "I am

Tradition." And when, taking leave at the end of the council, the archbishop prostrated himself to kiss the papal slipper, Pius IX rudely placed his foot on the nape of his neck and, putting his weight on it, cried out: "A stiff-necked fellow!"

In 1875, in the midst of the Church's struggle with Bismarck (*Kulturkampf*), Pius IX, in a letter to the German bishops in which he sanctioned the explanation they had given of the 1870 dogma, could only qualify this dogma in an ambiguous manner lest he call into question its very foundations. The pope, said the Germans, was the Bishop of Rome and not of Breslau or Cologne, but he was "the pastor and leader of all the bishops and of all the faithful, and his papal power must be respected and listened to everywhere and always, and not just in special and exceptional cases."[11]

The dialectic of primacy and collegiality ended on this occasion in absurdity: that the dogma of papal infallibility could only be defined in the context of a council seemed a pure contradiction. "As if the pope," wrote Alexis van Bunnen in an unpublished work, "had needed the council in order to declare infallibly that he had never needed it."[12]

To a certain popular religious mindset (but also among intellectuals), the pope appeared henceforth as "the only person in whom others saw a direct link to God," "as the man who represents the Son of God on earth. As such he acts in the stead and place of the second person of the almighty trinitarian God,"[13] and we see the myth of the center absorbing to its profit that of the Priest-King, the only mediator between humanity and the heavenly powers.[14]

# Notes

1. *Regestorum sive epistolarum* I, PL 214, 292A.
2. P. de Vooght, *Les pouvoirs du concile et l'autorité du Pape au concile de Constance* (Paris, 1965), pp. 170 and 173.
3. *Controversia* V, c. 4.
4. *De controversiis Christianæ Fidei nostri temporis* II, bk. 3, chapt. 2.
5. See Gregory of Nyssa's vigorous criticisms of pilgrimages to "the Holy Land."
6. Denzinger, 3064.
7. Denzinger, 3052, 3050, 3065.
8. Denzinger, 3061.
9. Mansi, 52, 338.
10. Mansi, 52, 678.
11. Text of the declaration of the German bishops approved in 1875 by Pius IX. See Dom O. Rousseau, "La vraie valeur de l'épiscopat dans l'Église d'après d'importants documents de 1875," *Irénikon* 29 (1956): 121–142.
12. *Les apories logiques du dogme de l'infaillibilité pontificale*, no date.
13. Vittorio Messori, in his interviews with John Paul II, published under the title *Entrez dans l'espérance* (Paris, 1994), pp. 17 and 25.
14. One can find similar phenomena, even less sophisticated, in the veneration accorded to the bishop in some regions of the Orthodox Church, where, for example, people prostrate themselves in front of him as he walks, in the hope of being touched by the sole of his shoe.

# 9.

# The "Orthodox" Reaction

The separation of 1054 is unquestionably linked to the rise of the "Gregorian reform." The reaction of Byzantine theologians remained for a long time moderate and open, never questioning the reality of Peter's presence in Rome or the primacy of that see. In the eleventh century, Theophylact of Ohrid concluded in his commentary on Luke 22:32–33: "It is on Peter and no other, and on him alone, that the Lord conferred the leadership of the entire flock of the universe."[1] Nicodemus, metropolitan of Nicodemia, responding to the arguments in favor of the papacy proposed by Anselm of Havelberg at the time of the controversy at Constantinople in 1136, agreed: "We possess here, in the archives of Hagia Sophia, the account of the exalted deeds of the Roman pontiffs; we have the Acts of the councils which set out everything you have said concerning the authority of the Roman Church. That is why it would redound to our shame if we were to deny what we see with our own eyes, as it was written by our Fathers."[2] The great fifteenth-century liturgist, Simeon of Thessalonica, likewise recalled that before the division the holy popes were always venerated by the Greek Church. He even accepted the list, then current in Rome, that made Peter the first bishop of the see: "With Popes Peter, Linus,

Clement, Stephen, Hippolytus, Sylvester, Innocent, Leo, Agapet, Martin, Agathon, and other popes, we enjoy communion in Christ, and we have no reason to separate ourselves from them. It is evident, since we celebrate their memory, calling them Doctors and Fathers. . . ."[3]

Generally speaking, Byzantine theologians saw a true analogy between the place of Peter among the apostles and the place of the bishop of Rome among the bishops. However, they questioned whether the pope had not momentarily departed from the faith of Peter, both in wanting to impose the *filioque* on the East, and in substantially modifying his own role in the Church. The same Nicodemus also wrote that, "The bishop of Rome should neither be called 'prince of the priesthood' nor 'supreme priest (*pontifex maximus*)' nor anything similar, but only the bishop of the first see. . . . The church of Rome, whose primacy among her sister churches we do not contest, to whom we acknowledge the first place with presidence at ecumenical councils, has separated herself through her own pretensions. . . . If the Roman Pontiff, sitting on the sublime throne of his glory, wants to fulminate against us and hurl orders at us from the heights of his sublimity, if he wants to judge our churches, not only with our counsel, but according to his opinion alone, as he desires, what brotherhood, indeed what fatherhood, could there be in that? Who could accept such a thing? For then we could not be called, nor would we any longer be, children of the Church, but veritable slaves. But the truth of Christ brings us to birth in the womb of the Church not for servitude but for freedom."[4]

Taking up the warnings of Christ in the gospel, the East called on Peter to repent and weep so that he might rediscover his true place in the Church. Theophilact placed these words in the mouth of Jesus speaking to Peter: "Because I made you the leader of my disciples, you will strengthen the others when you have wept and repented."[5] And Nicodemus wrote: "If the pope wants to have collaborators in the Lord's vineyard, let him live in the humility of his primacy and not despise his brothers."[6] Simeon of Thessalonica said much the same thing: "When the Latins affirm that the bishop of Rome is the first, they should not be contradicted. . . . Let them but show us that he remains in the faith of Peter and his successors, that he possesses what comes from Peter, then he will be the first, the chief shepherd and head of all, the supreme Pontiff. . . . If there should come such a one as resembles [the popes of the early Church] by the creed, by his life, by the morals of orthodoxy, he will be our common Father. We will take him to be Peter, and the bonds of union will last forever."[7]

Throughout these texts, one senses the certitude that there is only one Church but that within it there are serious problems. While waiting for a true council of union, always considered a possibility, the councils convoked by the Latin Church are in no way binding on the Greek Church. "When, prompted by circumstance, the Roman Church gathers in council with its western bishops, without our presence, it is right that its bishops accept and observe the decrees with due veneration. . . . But as for us, although we are not in disagreement with the Roman Church on the foundation of the catholic faith, how could we, since we do not hold these councils along with them, accept the decisions taken without our opinion and about which we ourselves know nothing?"[8]

At the beginning of the thirteenth century, the separation and the new Roman ecclesiology imprinted their mark on tragic events: the sack of Constantinople and the dismembering of the Byzantine Empire, the appointment by Pope Innocent III of a Latin patriarch of

Constantinople, the Venetian Thomas Morosini, and the "latinizing" activities of this patriarch. These events initiated, or at the least accentuated, in the East a violent, anti-Roman polemic, fueled over time by what the East saw as economic, political, cultural and religious aggression on the part of the West. The merchant republics of Italy and certain Frankish barons exploited and colonized the Byzantine world.[9] The council of union of Ferrara-Florence, 1438–1439, at the very moment when the Turks were overwhelming the Greek Empire and when the emperor was ready for any concession, became for the Orthodox Church, thanks to some verbal acrobatics, a council of capitulation, which monks and people promptly rejected. Other contributary factors were the inadequate help given by the West during the final assault on Constantinople; the formation in the sixteenth century of two henceforth separate confessions between which a council of union seemed unthinkable, and which in turn led to the annexation by Rome of vast Orthodox territories under the cover of uniatism; the multiplication of Latin missionaries in the Ottoman Empire who resorted to re-baptism from the beginning of the eighteenth century (after centuries of sporadic *communicatio in sacris*); the support given in the Levant to these missionaries by the embassies of Catholic countries; Italian attempts at Latinization in the Dodecanese, which continued until the end of World War II, and, during this war, the massacre of tens, indeed hundreds of thousands of Serbs by Croat nationalists under the guise of a so-called Catholic crusade: all events that fed the fear and mistrust of the Orthodox. The list could go on.

Let us recall the points at issue: the denial of the primacy of the person of Peter and the affirmation that the Church is built solely on his confession of faith; the consequent refusal of the petrine charism to the see of Rome, which reduced Roman primacy in the early Church to a mere matter of ecclesiastical law; a minimalist interpretation of *"primus inter pares,"* according to which the bishop of Rome had enjoyed only a position of honor among equals. All these arguments were reinforced in the sixteenth and seventeenth centuries by the Protestant polemic which, at one point, as we know, went so far as to identify the pope with the antichrist. In effect, Protestants and Orthodox collaborated in Poland and Lithuania to stop the expansion of the Counter Reformation, and, at the beginning of the seventeenth century, the great patriarch of Constantinople, Cyril Loukakis, resorted freely to Calvinist thought in order to rouse from its often superstitious inertia a sizeable part of the Orthodox world lying paralyzed in the wardship of Islam. In the nineteenth century, when the idea of Moscow as the "third Rome"[10] resurfaced among the Russian Christian intellegentia, the great slavophiles, Dostoyevsky among them, feared that the pope had given in to the temptations which had confronted Christ in the desert.

Faced with the preparation and subsequent promulgation of the dogma of Vatican I, the encyclical of the eastern patriarchs, who foregathered with their synods in 1848, as also the encyclical of the patriarch and synod of Constantinople in 1895, affirmed that "popery" as a "claim to domination" was a heresy[11] and that only the Church as a whole is indefectible: "The protector of religion consists in the entire body of the Church, that is, in the people themselves who want to preserve their faith intact." Among these, the bishops are the Church's "judges" and the laity its "shield." And the encyclical calls once again for "the tears of Peter."[12]

Thus the grave mistrust aroused by the attacks of Rome and the polemic which ensued, and perhaps also a kind of inferiority-superiority complex with regard to the West, have led to a certain amnesia in the Orthodox tradition, regarding an aspect of the patristic Tradition relevant to the presence of Peter at Rome and the possible service to be rendered to unity and universality by the bishop of that see.

Until the end of the nineteenth century, the patriarchate of Constantinople, *altera Roma* (the other Rome), functioned, at the very heart of the Orthodox Church, as a kind of temporary substitute for Rome, whose former role was thus acknowledged. At the council of 1592, after the establishment of the patriarchate of Moscow, the "apostolic Throne" of Constantinople declared itself to be "head and primate of the other patriarchates." The patriarchal and synodal Tome of 1663 contains the following question and response: "Can an appeal against the judgment of any other Church be brought before the throne of Constantinople, and can the latter resolve every ecclesiastical matter? Response: This privilege was that of the pope before the Church was torn asunder by presumptions and ill will. But since the Church is split apart, all the affairs of the churches are brought before the throne of Constantinople, which gives judgment, for, according to the canons, it enjoys the same primacy as the Rome of former times." Observe the extremely honest language concerning the schism.

However, the importance assumed by the Russian Church and the growing sense of nationality have transformed the Orthodox Church *de facto* into a grouping of national churches united, indeed, by faith, the sacrament and canonical tradition, but nevertheless increasingly independent of each other. The autocephalous church is sanctioned by tradition: it consists of local churches—in the sense of eucharistic communities—which, when grouped together, are granted the right to elect their own primate.

That is precisely what was defined by Nicaea in 325 with regard to the "metropolitan" province (canons 4 and 6). There followed the great patriarchates of the Pentarchy. But it was always a question of *interdependence* within a flexible hierarchy of primacies. By contrast, the autocephalism of the national churches in the nineteenth and twentieth centuries, influenced by a shift of feeling toward a secular nationalism, has tended toward an almost complete independence, a veritable religious nationalism, featuring often, within its own context, relations between the center and the bishops which differ little from Roman practice. Finally, at a council held in 1872 at Constantinople, what remained of the Pentarchy condemned as its last act a heresy known as "phyletism." It was defined as "the formation of particular churches which receive only believers of the same nationality, while excluding those of other nationalities."

Two councils—Vatican I in 1870 and Constantinople in 1872—with two attitudes to language: the first vindicated brazenly a debatable practice; the other threw a cloak of verbal integrity over a practice no less debatable, but inversely so. How then can the two sides reach an understanding and possibly complete each other?

## Notes

1. Theophylact, *Ennaratio in Evangelium Joannis*, PG 124, 309 A.
2. Nicodemus, *Dialogi*, PL 188, 1219.
3. Simeon of Thessalonica, *Dialogus contra haereses*, PG 155, 120–121.
4. Nicodemus, *Dialogi*, PL 188, 1219.
5. Ibid.
6. Ibid.
7. Simeon of Thessalonica, *Dialogus contra haereses*, PG 155, 120–121.
8. Nicodemus, *Dialogi*, PL 188, 1219.

9. But not all: the twelfth Latin Emperor of Constantinople, Henry, Count of Flanders, saved the Orthodox clergy from Roman persecution and preserved the monasteries of Athos.

10. Appearing at the beginning of the sixteenth century, after the fall of Constantinople, in a context of eschatalogical emotionalism, this theme was formally condemned by the councils of Moscow of 1666–1667.

11. Paragraph 13 of the encyclical of 1848.

12. Mansi, 40, 407–408. It is necessary to note that the encyclical never questions the ecclesiality of the Catholic Church, for it makes an appeal to the bishops and theologians of this Church.

# 10.

# Hope against Hope: The Challenge to Rome

In the course of a thousand years of history the see of Rome, while safeguarding the traditional ecclesial principle of her primacy, has increasingly interpreted this primacy as absolute power over the Church. Orthodoxy, meanwhile, feeling rightly or wrongly that anything Latin could only be out to destroy it, gradually moved from a denial of "popery," that is, the mediaeval and especially the modern exercise of primacy, to a virtual denial of this primacy as the presence of Peter in the Church. Simplistically put, Peter has been parted from his brothers, the apostles, and they have been parted from him. In consequence, while the Church on both sides remains faithful to Christ as the Truth and the Life, she must admit she has lost to some degree the multiple fine-tuned aerials that allowed her to perceive him as the Way.

Our hope—and that of so many Christians—transcends the vicissitudes and the seeming backtrackings of history: it is the hope that Rome, when God wills it, and by an operation of grace unique to her, will return to the authentic conception of primacy as the servant of communion, within a framework of genuine interdependence between her bishop and all other bishops, and also of real dialogue with the entire people of God. It will require the integration of her own reformed churches (which will remind her that she must be the Church of Peter *and* Paul), as well as reconciliation, as between two sister-churches and without any juridical pretensions, with the Orthodox Church. The latter, for its part, while preserving the teaching of the Fathers on the freedom of sister-churches within the universal Church, will have to overcome the temptation of autocephalism and religious nationalism in order to rediscover exactly how collegiality and primacy interconnect, while not forgetting what the East had fully recognized during the first millennium: that, once unity of faith is re-established, primacy will remain indivisibly founded on the person and faith of Peter, on a petrine ministry balanced by that of Paul, the charismatic, as well as by that of John, the visionary.

Signs of "conversion" on Peter's part have multiplied during the second half of the twentieth century. Paul VI abandoned the tiara, one of whose crowns symbolized supreme temporal power and the other spiritual. He also wanted his funeral to take place in the utmost simplicity. John Paul I and then John Paul II also renounced the tiara and the rite of coronation. But the most significant sign by far remains the Second Vatican Council. Its very convocation weakened the dogma of 1870 that seemed to render useless and even theologically impossible the holding of a council.

With some encouragement from the East (whether Uniate or Orthodox), Vatican II gave back to the episcopal ministry its full sacramentality and re-established the common collegial responsibility of the pope and the bishops for guiding the universal Church. Despite the *Nota explicativa praevia* of 16 November 1964, which, due to a reaction of fear and the desire for continuity, affirmed that episcopal collegiality was always exercised *sub Petro et cum Petro* (this note, however, is not a conciliar document in the strict sense), it is the ministry of the bishop and not that of the pope, as was the case in 1870, which the council designated as "ordinary," "immediate," exercised "personally in the name of Christ." "Pastoral responsibility, that is, the habitual, daily care of the flock, is returned fully [to the bishops]. They should not be considered as vicars of the Roman pontiffs, for they exercise a power which is proper to them and they truly are the leaders of the people whom they guide." They are, therefore, for their respective churches, the "vicars and legates of Christ."[1] Being divinely instituted, the bishops therefore "govern the house of the living God."[2] The "Constitution on the Church" no longer goes from the pope to the bishops, but from the bishops to the pope. Christ has built his Church not on Peter alone but on all the apostles with Peter as their head, and so today, not on the pope alone but on the college of bishops with the successor of Peter as their head.[3] Out of the nineteen passages of this "Constitution" that speak of the ministry of the pope, only one bears the former juridical stamp. All the others bear witness to an authentic rediscovery of a spiritual understanding of primacy. The emphasis is placed on the patristic theme, principally developed by Cyprian of Carthage, that the successor of Peter bodies forth the unity of the episcopacy, the unity of the Church, primacy being a foundation of unity of faith and communion.[4]

The universal Church is defined as a communion of local churches each one of which is founded upon the eucharist. The highest manifestation of the Church consists in the full and active participation of all the holy people of God at the same liturgical celebrations, above all at the same eucharist.[5] That is why the role of the bishop of Rome is "to preside in charity" (as Ignatius of Antioch puts it) over all the diversity of the individual churches.[6]

Jurisdiction is based on sacrament and not on some independent source. The new Code of Canon Law of the Catholic Church, promulgated in 1983, has clearly renounced the classic binomial of order and jurisdiction.

As there is no sacrament of papacy, the foundation of papal power rests on the fact that the pope is bishop of Rome. His ministry, therefore, can only be understood within the framework of the exercise of episcopacy. However extensive might be the "solicitude" that falls to his charge, it can only operate within the context of episcopal grace.[7]

The canonical order of the Church no longer derives from the pope, though he may reserve to himself certain exceptional cases which concern the good of the entire Church. The bishops enjoy in their dioceses all the power required for the exercise of their pastoral charge. However, the Roman pontiff can, by virtue of his responsibility, reserve to himself certain cases or reserve them to another such authority.[8]

Putting the decisions of a council into practice requires many years, even decades. Such was the case of the First Ecumenical Council in 325, which did not fully become a part of the Church's tradition until 381. As we shall see in the next chapter, Paul VI entered on an in-depth dialogue with the Orthodox. Faithful to the spirit of Vatican II, he permitted the organization of episcopal conferences. Their grouping by continents conjured up a fleeting vision of patriarchates. But things became more complex with John Paul II. Whatever his original dispositions, John Paul II has been deeply marked by his collision with the Marxian influence (Marxian rather than Marxist, but he has failed to make the distinction—a measure of his lack of fully under-standing it) permeating certain currents of Catholic thought. He has been shocked above all by the adventuring, the extreme audacity, the doubts that have characterized Christian thought in the Western world, a world in which he lost no time diagnosing, like the monks of Mount Athos, "a culture of death." In contrast to the spirit of Vatican II, he availed himself of his *plenitudo potestatis* to safeguard what he took to be the very foundations of the faith, and which he expressed in a synthesis made up of neo-thomism combined with a certain germanic phenomenology. Some bishops were passed over; others were put forward. The role of episcopal conferences was diminished, and the synod set up at the pope's side was reduced to a purely advisory body at the service of the primatial office. The many diocesan synods have certainly been able to deliberate freely, but such demands as went against the stand taken by Rome (e.g., the ordination of married men) have been set aside without comment.

It is clear that his own personal style, the capacity of a powerful personality to appeal directly to the crowds and to command the television screen by the density of his prayer and his faith, have worried non-Catholics by giving renewed importance to the psychological and historical role of the papacy. At the same time John Paul II has seemed more and more open to Orthodoxy in recent years. There is no doubt that he shares with Orthodoxy a certain abhor-rence of western civilization as well as an emphatic and uncomplicated attachment to the fundamental truths of the faith. Indeed, words and gestures that indicate a wish for reconciliation and convergence have multiplied since 1993. In June of that year, the great Catholic-Orthodox commission, gathered at the University of Balamand in north Lebanon, affirmed that "the two Churches are sisters" and condemned uniatism and proselytism. The pope's Lenten retreat in 1994 was given by Fr. Spidlik, who has a deep and refined knowledge of both Orthodox spirituality and the world view of Russian Christianity.[9] In this same year it was the patriarch of Constantinople who was asked to furnish the text of the *Via Crucis*, read by the pope on Good Friday. The apostolic letter *Orientale Lumen* ("The Light of the East") appeared in 1995 and reflected a remarkable grasp of the spiritual sensibilities of the East (and of the undivided Church). It was followed by the great encyclical on ecumenism, *Ut unum sint*, and the "Doctrinal Note" concerning the procession of the Holy Spirit.

In the encyclical, it is the acknowledgment that "sanctification and truth" exist in other Christian traditions that underlies and justifies the ecumenical process. If the Church is holy in Gospel and eucharist, she is often a sinner in her human—all too human—dimension, which is why the ecumenical process must start with conversion to the gospel and repentance. The pope, like the apostle Peter, must be the first to repent, and the Catholic Church along with him. Here at last is the response to Orthodoxy's long-hoped-for "tears of Peter." The ecclesiology of communion is reaffirmed and presented as an analogy of trinitarian communion. Grace, expressed no longer in thomistic language but in that of scripture and the Fathers, is presented as a real participation in divine life. But most importantly, at the end of the encyclical the problem of primacy is the object of a moving address in which the pope indicts himself, acknowledging that the petrine ministry is that of the pardoned sinner, a humble opening to grace. This was followed by an invitation to "ecclesiastical leaders and theologians to engage in fraternal and patient dialogue with me on this subject, a dialogue in which our mutual listening might transcend empty polemic, with nothing other in mind than Christ's will for his Church."

In an address delivered to Patriarch Bartholomew I on 29 June 1995, John Paul II, speaking of the problem of the procession of the Holy Spirit (*filioque*) declared: "The Father, as source of the entire Trinity, is the sole origin of the Son and of the Holy Spirit." This is precisely the Orthodox position. The Doctrinal Note of 13 September 1995 sought to ground its whole development on the trinitarian faith of the creed of Nicaea-Constantinople in its original text. "The Holy Spirit originates from the Father alone, as from his first principle, of himself and without intermediary." The Note does not hesitate to take up the formula of Patriarch Photius, according to whom "the Spirit proceeds from the Father alone," while observing that it is insofar as he is the Father of the only Son. In the end, it is not a question of denying the Latin tradition, but of showing that there are two differing approaches, of which both are legitimate and neither in any way contradicts the other.

## Notes

1. *Lumen Gentium*, 27.
2. Ibid., 18
3. Ibid., 22.
4. Ibid., 18.
5. Ibid., 26.
6. Ibid.
7. Ibid., 21.
8. Ibid., 23.
9. See his *Idée russe* (Troyes, 1995).

# 11.

# Hope against Hope:
# The Challenge to Orthodoxy

The Orthodox Church, for its part, is called to overcome its fear, mistrust and isolation. During the sixties the prophetic patriarch of Constantinople, Athenagoras I, pointed out the pathway to the future. In his opinion, only a reunited Christianity would be able to respond to the twofold challenge of our time: on the one hand, the unification of the planet, and, on the other, the passionate intensification of differences, through the trinitarian meaning of otherness within unity.

In Athenagoras' view, the fundamental split in the history of Christianity was the one that occurred between East and West at the beginning of the second millennium. That split, he said, set off a chain reaction of disintegration, and it was this that needed healing, beginning with Rome and Constantinople, the two protagonists. In this way Christianity would achieve reintegration through a reverse chain reaction. Orthodoxy would be freed to reenter the historical process, and the Christian West would escape the opposite temptation: to fuse with that process its identity dispersed among sects and eastern religions. Rome and the Reformation, thanks in part to the Orthodox catalyst, would re-engage without losing either the sense of liberty or that of mystery.

A year after Athenagoras and Paul VI met in Jerusalem, the anathemas exchanged in 1054 were lifted, allowing the opening of a "dialogue of charity" between the two churches, a dialogue that affirmed their "effective will to reach a common understanding of the apostolic faith and its demands." In July 1967, Paul VI came to Istanbul and, as a sign of atonement, prayed at Hagia Sophia, on the very spot where, in 1054, a cardinal had excommunicated the ecumenical patriarch in the name of the see of Rome (unoccupied at the time, although the cardinal did not know it, following the death of Pope Leo IX). Receiving Paul VI at the Phanar, Athenagoras greeted him as "the very holy successor of Peter."[1]

When the patriarch in turn came to Rome,[2] he acknowledged that the bishop of Rome was "the bearer of the apostolic grace and the successor of a constellation of holy and wise men who have made this see illustrious, this see which is the first in honor and rank in the living body of Christian churches spread throughout the world, and whose holiness, wisdom and struggles on behalf of the common faith of the undivided Church are a permanent possession and a treasure of the entire Christian world."[3]

In March 1971, in a message brought to Rome by his friend and adviser, Metropolitan Meliton, the patriarch declared that he saw the bishop of Rome as "the elder brother," "the herald and eminent artisan of the peace, love and unity of Christians."[4] In a spontaneous gesture that overwhelmed the metropolitan, Paul VI fell at his feet and embraced them, the opposite gesture—and how symbolic— of Pius IX putting his weight on the neck of the Latin patriarch of Antioch, who in 1870 had dared to oppose the dogma of Vatican I.

The dialogue between Athenagoras and Paul VI, in which one could feel their friendship growing, has been recorded in the *Tomos Agapis* (*The Book of Love*) and published simultaneously in 1971 by the Phanar and the Vatican. It remains for today and still more for tomorrow a true *locus theologicus*, a theological meeting-point. The pope and the patriarch emphasized the existence of a common language between the two sister-churches, that of the Apostles and that of the Fathers, as well as over a thousand years of experience as an undivided Church. Paul VI placed the emphasis on the local church as eucharistic community. "In each local church the mystery of divine love is at work. Is this not why the local churches loved calling themselves by the traditional and most beautiful expression of sister-churches"?[5] From this perspective of an ecclesiology of communion, the patriarch, for his part, stressed that it was not the mystery of Roman primacy that was questioned by the Orthodox, only some of its modern applications. Time and again he used the expression of Ignatius of Antioch, speaking of a "presidency of love" vested in the church of Rome. Thus, despite the Roman doctrine of primacy as formulated in 1870 by Vatican I and by *Nota proevia* in 1964, Athenagoras I recognized the petrine (and pauline) mystery of the see of Rome, a charism always present, inhering, independently of all theorizing, in experiential practice. Indeed, in 1974, on the occasion of the seventh centenary of the Council of Lyon (a council of union which failed in its purpose), Paul VI made a clear distinction between the true ecumenical councils, that is, the seven held in common by both East and West in the first millennium and the "general" councils, convoked by the Latin Church after the separation, and which are valid only for her (an affirmation taken up many times since by Cardinal Ratzinger).

John Paul II adopted this same language of sister-Churches (which Ratzinger had meanwhile put under severe strain), when he made his first visit to non-Catholics by going to Constantinople in 1979. The dialogue between the two Churches, no longer simply one "of charity" but theological in the proper sense, finally got under way the following year, and a joined commission, meeting at intervals, produced some important documents concerning both the sacramental structure of the Church and the problem of the "Greek Catholic" Churches.

Bartholomew I, before his election as patriarch, served eight years as vice-president of a commission of the eucumenical council called "Faith and Constitution," the only commission where Catholics were fully represented. Without a doubt, it is within those walls that shared reflection has made the greatest progress over the last twenty years, a progress characterized by integrity. He is, therefore, particularly well informed about ecumenical problems and has a knowledge of contemporary exegesis that Athenagoras lacked.

On several occasions he has adverted to "our elder brother, Pope John Paul II," "the bishop of the first see of Rome with whom we are in a communion of love." However, he has quickly gone on to say that there would be no progress toward unity without "fear of God, sincerity and prudence."

The collapse of communism and the ensuing invasion of its territories by the most objectionable by-products of western culture have led in many Orthodox milieux to an identity crisis that is violently anti-Western and anti-Catholic. In the countries of eastern and south-eastern Europe, these Orthodox communities (there are others as well) have joined in the general uprising of the East in its many guises against the West. And if, for Islam, the West most often means Christianity, for this segment of

Orthodoxy, whose influence outweighs its size, West means Rome. The Yugoslavian crisis has resurrected the specter of a Catholic-Islamic alliance (1204 and 1453) bent on the destruction of the Orthodox world.

Patriarch Bartholomew knew how to confront what he termed "anti-Catholic hysteria" and on more than one occasion he saved the dialogue without, however, after being weakened by the 1996 conflict with Moscow, being able to prevent the (unexplained) cancellation by the Orthodox of the scheduled meeting of the joined commission. Although he was clearly in agreement with the Vatican on viewing the *filioque* problem in proper perspective (in June of 1995 in Zurich he recalled with humor how Einstein had expounded the laws of relativity in that city), by the spring of that same year he was strongly criticizing Rome's interpretation of the famous passage of Matthew 16:18, "You are Peter, the rock, and on this rock I will build my Church." The meeting in Rome between Bartholomew I and John Paul II, on 27–29 June 1995, was certainly rich in symbolic gestures: the benediction given in common and the final call of the patriarch to the faithful, "Courage, let us love one another!" It was, however, a failure as a meeting of minds. The two men agreed that the exercise of primacy only makes sense as service and requires the utmost humility. But the patriarch underscored how complex and controversial the interpretation of Matthew 16:18 had been and still was. The pope for his part said little in reply. His real response is found at the end of his encyclical *Ut unum sint*, which calls for ecumenical reflection on the exercise of papal primacy.

Again in Zurich, on 14 December 1995, Bartholomew stated unambiguously that the only authority of divine origin existing in the Church was that of the bishops and their collegiality, and that the pope's role had no scriptural foundation. At the end of June 1996, in an interview for the Polish weekly, *Tygodnik Powszechny*, the patriarch reaffirmed that "the ministry of the pope has become the biggest and most scandalous stumbling block" to dialogue between Orthodox and Roman Catholics. Moreover, he questioned the exercise of this ministry since the end of the first millennium, notably "the mistaken theological claims" to universal papal jurisdiction.

For Bartholomew, the mission given by Christ to Peter was in reality given to each bishop and to the bishops collectively, as being the successors of the Twelve, and not to the bishop of Rome alone. All the bishops are collegially the successors of all the apostles. Indeed no serious exegete today would maintain that Peter received the order to "govern" the other apostles. If he is the first, it is among his equals. Vatican II, as we have seen, recognized that the petrine ministry could only function within the grace sustaining the episcopacy, for there is no sacrament of papacy.

Even though getting things out on the table is indispensable for today's reflection on the subject, these objections could well seem somewhat reductive and polemical. Criticism of the ways in which Roman primacy is exercised is certainly called for, especially if it is a question of the mediaeval and modern forms mentioned in the interview with the Polish weekly. But at the same time it is important to recall the "mystery" of the presence of Peter (and Paul) in Rome, and the "presidency of love" vested in consequence in the church of that city, a mystery fully recognized by the East from the fifth century, and indeed to recall too the special role of Peter (*protos* and not *arché*) which the New Testament attests.

How to explain the intransigent positions taken by the patriarch? I would propose, very tentatively, two hypotheses: on the one hand, there is, as I have said, a hardening of the reactionary stance in certain Orthodox camps, which he cannot overlook, and on the other, the admirable ecclesiology developed by one of his advisers, the very learned professor John Zizioulas, now Metropolitan John of Pergamum. In his magisterial book, *L'Eucharistie, l'évêque et l'unité de l'Église,*[6] Zizioulas sees no other structure of grace in the Church than that of the episcopacy; the rest is the product of history. This is in contrast to this century's other great Orthodox ecclesiologist, Father Nicholas Afanassieff, who was a professor at the Institute Saint Serge of Paris: the latter descried that from the very earliest years of the Church, a greater "priority of reception" was accorded to the church of Rome.

In this context of uncertainty, let us conclude by recalling a prophetic event that took place recently in the Middle East, in the antiochene era. At the time of the Synod of the Greek Catholic Church held in Lebanon, from 24 July to 4 August 1995, nearly all the bishops signed a profession of faith, which consisted in the following two points: (1) I believe everything which the Orthodox Church teaches. (2) I am in communion with the bishop of Rome, in the role that the Eastern Fathers accorded him before the separation.

This text was in fact approved by one of the greatest bishops of the Orthodox patriarchate of Antioch, Metropolitan George Khodr', with the agreement of the patriarch himself, Ignatius IV Hazim. George Khodr' declared, "I consider this profession of faith to set the necessary and sufficient conditions for re-establishing the unity of the Orthodox Churches with Rome." One should not look for any results, other than extremely modest ones, during the antiochene era. The elderly Greek Catholic patriarch of Antioch, prudently, did not sign the declaration. The Vatican has remained silent and the pope himself seems to know nothing about it. On the Orthodox side, the integralists are wary. The autocephalic Churches maintain a determined silence. But regardless, the healing over of wounds has begun, and no longer just in the heart; for the first time its possibility is foreseen in the very structures of the Church. Let us not forget that it was at Antioch that the disciples of Jesus were first called Christians!

## Notes

1. *Tomos Agapis* (*The Book of Love*), Constantinople-Rome, 1971, p. 378.
2. Paul VI went first to Istanbul lest the visit of Athenagoras to Rome be interpreted by some of the Orthodox as a gesture of submission.
3. *Tomos Agapis*, p. 413.
4. Ibid., p. 619.
5. Ibid.
6. Paris: Desclée de Brouwer, 1994.

# 12.

# The Mystery of Primacy

The foundation of all primacy in the Church is Christ and Christ alone—crucified and risen, the conqueror of death *by means of death*. Christ is the only high priest of the new covenant, to whom all authority in heaven and on earth belongs. It is significant that the New Testament only uses the word *hiéreus*, high priest in biblical Greek, with respect to Christ on the one hand, and to the entire people of God on the other.

All primacy within redeemed humanity—basically that of the bishop in the local church, but also that of the metropolitan among his bishops, of the patriarch among metropolitans, and finally that of the first bishop, the bishop of Rome, within the Pentarchy at the time of the undivided Church—is a precarious image (ever in need of refining) of the primacy of Christ, the one whom Father Lev Gillet, writing as "a monk of the Eastern Church," called "Lord Love."[1] It is the primacy of service that extends, should need be, to witnessing through the shedding of blood and through death.

I do not care much for Saint Peter's Basilica in Rome, with its colossal and empty mass, its almost naïve pride. However, the excavated area beneath Saint Peter's, recently brought to light, has a significant humility about it.

It must have been a peripheral Roman road with tombs to either side, for the dead in antiquity, whether cremated or buried, were kept far from the living. One of these tombs is perhaps that of Peter. No one knows for sure, because in the course of the excavations, obviously carried out from the top down, there was a certain amount of caving in, but some bones were discovered wrapped in a blood-stained cloth. Orthodox leaders visiting Rome all come to pray before this tomb. In fact, the true Saint Peter's is underground, and to grasp this is to understand how, during the first centuries, the church of Rome was venerated as the church of the martyr-apostles Peter and Paul, then as that of the martyr-bishops, and that its true role could only be one of *martyria*—in the special double sense of witness and martyrdom. Athenagoras I recognized that in 1971, and it is still true today.

Primacy has another foundation: namely Christ's teaching in John's Gospel on the unity of the disciples as based on the love of the Father and the Son, in other words, trinitarian love. The principle of unity in God is the Person of the Father. It is the mystery of a Fatherhood both sacrificial and liberating. "Ever moving repose," says Maximus the Confessor, where the Father gives all that he is while at the same time securing the circumincession—and the bestowal upon humanity—of Life and Love. Not that the Father produces the other Persons; that would be a reified interpretation of his "monarchy." He places himself while giving them their place. He makes himself, like them, responsible for a communion for which *his* responsibility is primary. Canon 34 (the so-called "apostolic" canon) comes once again to mind: "It is fitting that the bishops should know who among them is the first and that they acknowledge him as head, and that they do nothing outside their own churches without having consulted with him. But neither should the one who is first do anything without deliberating with all the others. . . . In this way there will be unity of thought, and God will be glorified [God here means the Father] through the Lord in the Holy Spirit."

Need one add that it is in no way essential to the exercise of such a primacy that the bishop of Rome should appoint the bishops of the entire world, that his administrative headquarters should be a sovereign territory, and that he should be a head of state among all the powerful "who are given the title Benefactor," and in consequence maintain a diplomatic corps?[2]

It is possible to conceive of a Church restructured around dynamic eucharistic communities, each gathered round its bishop, yet linked, through different groupings, to centers of unison and of communion: metropolitan sees, patriarchates (their composition based often on nationality, but more and more on common culture and destiny), with universal primacy ultimately pertaining to the bishop of Rome as the embodiment of both the presence of Peter and the charismatic inspiration of Paul.

John Paul II, on a number of occasions, but always during private interviews, has spoken of a primatial authority "with different gears," which would fully respect, as the Antiochenes propose, the internal freedom of the eastern Churches, as it existed during the first millennium (this would no doubt entail some very major adjustments in the relationships between Rome and a number of the reformed churches). Hasn't the present pope also said in identical circumstances, "What I seek with the Orthodox is communion not jurisdiction"?

It would undoubtedly be necessary to specify that infallibility—or rather, regarding the essence of the faith, indefectiblility—is conferred exclusively by the Holy Spirit, who, as we have said, is perceived in a variety of ways in the Church, and therefore that the definitions formulated *ex cathedra* by the bishop of Rome express the concrete communion of the Church. The dogma of Vatican I makes it clear, moreover, that it is not the pope himself who is infallible, but his definitions, and this by the particular assistance of the Holy Spirit. As such they would have an intrinsic validity and would not require confirmation by the Church, as it might be democratically. At the same time, however, it has to be admitted that the expression "*non ex consensu ecclesiae*" (not from the Church's consensus) is most unfortunate, and that it would be necessary to clarify the connection between these formulations and the entire ecclesial communion or, in other words, to foresee a link between the three forms of Peter's succession which we have indicated: the faith of the people of God, which can be expressed, on occasion, by a single prophet; the episcopacy in its collegiality, *in solidum*, as Cyprian of Carthage said; and finally the bishop of that church that was "founded and constituted" by the apostles Peter and Paul. This does not mean that the pope must be merely a spokesman, like the sovereign in a constitutional monarchy who "reigns without governing." A certain right of appeal (to be clari-fied, as in the case of the canons of Serdica); the adoption of positions that, while not decisive, would carry great weight (like the celebrated "Tomes" sent to ecumenical councils during the first millennium); the convocation of councils, which today the pope would be called upon to preside at and ratify—all these things would allow the pope to engage constructively both with moments of turbulence in public opinion and with hesitation and disagreements among the bishops. *The one essential would be to pass from a situation where the hierarchical dovetailing of power structures has legal back-up, to one where tensions are held in balance without predetermined juridical solutions.* In the first situation the opinion—if that is the word—of the People of God must "fit in," willy nilly, with the decisions of the bishops, which in turn must ultimately slot into the will of the pope, with all the *notae praeviae* necessary for "resolving" any conflict. Where tensions are held in balance, even in robust confrontations like that between Peter and Paul at Antioch, the last word belongs to none but the Holy Spirit, who cannot but bring forth agreement—a certitude of faith for all who put their confidence in the promises of Christ. However, in contrast to the world's political systems (even those which multiply the checks and balances, considering power to be a necessary evil) there can be no pre-established recipes—only prayer and, calling on the communion of saints, an asceticism of the mind, that it might be open to the prompting of the Holy Spirit. Not without humor, albeit of the bitter-sweet variety, we might recall that it has taken the Chalcedonians and the non-Chalcedonians[3] fourteen centuries to begin to realize that they are fundamentally in agreement.

I have already mentioned how Paul VI, in a message written in 1974, distinguished between the true ecumenical councils, held conjointly by East and West during the first millennium, and the general councils of the West, which, convoked after the separation of East and West, do not constrain the Orthodox. One could, therefore, proceed toward a common reflection, as John Paul II requested at the end of *Ut unum sint*, on decisions made during the centuries of division, and especially on a re-examination of the dogma of 1870, already partially balanced by Vatican II.

Should the pope fall bleeding in the triumphant and preposterous decor of Bernini, it is the underlying Saint

Peter's that would reappear, with the tradition of the apostles and the martyr-bishops. When John Paul II went, on his own initiative, to visit the patriarch of Constantinople, he knew the risk he was taking. Unambiguous threats had been made in extremist circles preparing the joint advance of the nationalist and islamic causes, circles that were already grooming the would-be murderer, whom the leaders of the communist world had little trouble making use of. The intended assassination attempt was simply deferred. It became the price to be paid for the visit to Constantinople, the sacrifice which gave to that visit a mystical dimension the importance of which will only gradually be revealed. For the blood then shed made without any doubt of the *Pontifex maximus* the *Servus servorum Dei*.

## Notes

1. See A Monk of the Eastern Church (Un moine de l'Église d'Orient), *Amour sans limites* (Chévetogne, 1971).

2. That the existence of the Vatican State guarantees the independence of the papacy is a myth. None of the great popes of the first eight centuries had at their command such a state. They bore witness to the independence of the Church through martyrdom if necessary. Today everything depends on the political and ideological situation of Italy and western Europe. If these found themselves directly in the hands of a Hitler or a Stalin, the pope would have no other recourse but silence, covert activity and finally martyrdom once again. During World War II, and despite the fact that Mussolini was not remotely comparable to Hitler, Pius XII maintained a prudent silence in the face of the tragedies taking place, concealing certain initiatives which became, virtually, "private."

3. The Chalcedonians (Catholics, Orthodox, and the majority of Protestants) acknowledge the dogma of the Council of Chalcedon (451), which says that the divine "nature" and the human "nature" unite in the one "person" of Christ, "without mixing, without change, without division or separation." The non-Chalcedonians (Armenians, Jacobites,

Copts, Ethiopians, South Indians) acknowledge but one divine-human nature of Christ. Obviously the word "nature" does not mean the same thing for each group, but the faith is the same, especially if one keeps in mind all the clarifications and corrections carried out by both sides in the course of the centuries that followed.

# Postscript: For a Common Future

*To Michelina T.*

The present times are strange. On the one hand the planet is unifying, but on the other, each ethnic group, each culture insists on its own identity and does so at the expense of others. Wars break out or threaten to do so. Will the future be made up of local wars—like all those which since the end of World War II have created an increasing number of victims (some say nearly sixty million)—or will they be wars between civilizations, as some American political analysts suggest, who have principally in mind the growing demographic weight of Islam?

This will no doubt be the pattern for a long time, which will not prevent the economic and technological unification of humanity. Then, one day, there will break out what Nietzsche called the great "wars of the spirit," of which we already see the foreshadowing. It is through the medium of these wars that I shall attempt to indicate what the spiritual foundations of our common future might be. For us Christians it will be in the light of the death and resurrection of Christ. And these foundations moreover are *duties:*

—the duty to transcend modernity through interiority.

—the duty to respond to the problem of evil.

—the duty to address theologically and spiritually the unity of the planet.

—the duty to create a new way of living.

## Transcending Modernity through Interiority

Modernity understood as freedom from clerical constraints has permitted remarkable explorations: from the nebulas of the cosmos to the infinitesimal particles of matter, of the human being body and soul—passing, as we used to say in jest, "from the man of the caverns to the caverns of man"—of art to the limits of subjectivity and folly, of politics as far as preliminary sketches, needing continual correction, of a "State of Rights," which never imposes a truth but allows the seeker to search and demonstrators to demonstrate freely.

In this sense modernity will last. Constraints on freedom can no longer be tolerated. However, freedom today is disquieted and self-questioning. Our first task is to commit ourselves to its inner movement in order to humbly give it a meaning, which will liberate it from emptiness. How? By the ultimate justification of existence; by giving science and technology a direction; by deepening our common solidarity.

1. Never has death been so naked and so intensely denied. Emptiness gnaws away at everything, incites derision, the search for some ultimate for which one will risk one's own life and the lives of others. On the desk of a student who had just committed suicide a note was found: "I'm killing myself, because life has no meaning." The foundation needing to be laid here is not the exaltation of

life—in the face of the void everyone exalts life, albeit strangely mixed with death, a living death, as Gregory of Nyssa called it—but the witness of resurrected life: in Christ, under the breath and fire of the Spirit, a space of non-death opens up before us. There are some who, pushing to the limit the "memory of death," discover in their own depths Someone who is forever interposing himself between humanity and the void: Christ risen, conqueror of death and hell. Therefore, one can risk loving and living. Eternal life begins now!

2. Giving a direction to science and technology. Contemporary humanity does not know what to do with its power. Sometimes science, or rather the sciences, are quite modest and do not pretend to define or exhaust reality as they come up against chaos; but sometimes (especially in biology) human prometheanism runs riot and claims the right to create life and fabricate humans on demand. The most profound symbolism concerning the union of man and woman, the relationship between parent and child, is cast aside. The blitzing of taboos reduces the human being to the level of a machine, needy, voracious, yet wholly isolated. Embryos are frozen only to be destroyed. Earth's natural rhythms are disregarded till nature itself is disfigured. The ugliness of our polluted cities is breeding violence.

The spiritual foundation which we need to lay here is two-fold: the transcendence of the person and the mystery of creation, the earth. An anthropology that is honest must acknowledge the irreducible character of the person, who is always more than his or her attributes and conditioning. The more I know someone the more he or she is unknown. Concepts are always transcended by a face, the face behind the mask, the many masks, the face glimpsed in the fault-line of a look, expressed in the life of a smile, of a presence which interrogates me and makes me respond, as Emmanuel Levinas has said. And what is more, we will have to make this understood: the human being is in the image of God. Like God, the human being is *hiddenness and love*. Neither science nor technology are of much value to those who deny or are not aware of the transcendence of the human person.

The mystery of humanity and the mystery of the earth. If the Bible and Christianity, the monks in particular, have rescued the human person from the impersonality of Mother Earth, the ancient Great Goddess, we must give up seeing the earth as either a more or less attractive backdrop or as an inexhaustible reserve of industrial energy, which is simply not the case. "Our sister, mother earth," said Francis of Assisi, our sister, our betrothed. Technological civilization must renew a nuptial contract with the earth. We must integrate into a renewed Christianity the great intuitions of the ancient pagan religions, such as the earth as theophany, or shall we say, as eucharist. Hence, by crossing horizontal knowledge, pure causal knowledge of things, with the vertical dimension, with its heavenly roots, science and technology can contribute to beautifying and spiritualizing it, while holding the earth in respect.

Solidarity is one of today's values which most attracts young people in the West. They show great dedication, especially in the "non-governmental organizations," not in simple individual gestures of charity, or in ideology quickly taken over by the state or by fanaticism, but they have a sense for what is practical and effective. However, they also risk becoming discouraged and embittered.

Our role is to deepen our solidarity-in-communion in the certainty that there exists one Person, one Adam ever broken by our sin, forever reconstituted in Christ, in whom we all have our being, "members of one another." And in this vast unity, each person, without trying is unique. It is God's common life communicating itself, the mystery of the trinitarian God, which Tarkovsky succeeded in suggesting at the end of his film on Andrei Roublev, while showing the icon of the Three Angels resplendent in light and color—a God symbolized by youth and beauty and who opens to humanity a future still strung out down all the centuries to come. There can no longer be discouragement or bitterness. In the Risen Christ even our failures are trans-figured. Each step we take in actively loving anticipates the Kingdom.

## Responding to the Problem of Evil

The fundamental argument of the atheism of today and tomorrow is that the existence of an all-powerful and good God is incompatible with the appalling reality of evil, which is not simply human—in which case one could blame it on human choice—but also cosmic. When a people so maltreated by history as the Armenians suffer all the conse-quences of a horrible earthquake, when infants in Mexico are buried in a landslide, when children here at home are stricken with cancer, everything seems absurd. One can sympathize with Ivan Karamozov, who lost his faith because of the suffering of innocent children. "You main-tain," they tell us, "that God is all powerful, and yet the world is an absurd chaos. You say that God is good, and yet he prepares for the countless damned an eternal torture chamber. Throughout history humans have killed one another in the name of God and still do today. You say that

God is merciful, yet it seems to us that he evokes cruelty and hatred." The French philosopher René Girard is correct in aligning violence and the sacred. Every community strengthens itself by denouncing a scapegoat. Every community works through certain exclusion mechanisms, and in the case of a religious community, these mechanisms are projected into eternity!

In this context what spiritual underpinning can one lay down as a basis for the future? It needs to be said unequivocally that our God is innocent, that God has not wanted and *does not want death*, that God does not even have the idea of evil. We must be rid of the notion of a diabolical God made in the image of humanity, humanity at its worst. A notion born from the stories of the wars, in part legendary, fought by the people of Israel when they moved into the land of Canaan, first to conquer then to preserve the "laboratory" of monotheism, a notion reinforced, in the theological history of the West, by the senile systematizations of an Augustine. It is a notion cultivated by the need of all those nominal Christians, so harshly criticized by Nietzsche, for vengeance or reparation.

Yes, there is a divine omnipotence, since God can create and allow other freedoms to exist outside himself, such as the freedom of the angels or of humanity. One Hebrew verb alone, *bara*, is used to describe this divine creation. We can create only reflections, puppets (and the philosophical concept of a God who has foreknowledge of all things, a conception which turns us into puppets, is certainly not biblical).

But at the same time it must be said that if there is a divine omnipotence, it is inseparable from God's equally infinite weakness. God is self-effacing, pulling back in some sense—the *tzimtzum* of Jewish mysticism—in order to allow the angel and the human being sufficient space for freedom. God awaits our love, but the love of another is not subject to control. "All great love is crucified," said Paul Evdokimov. Yes, God has risked, God has entered into a true and therefore tragic love story. Adam, the Adam that we all are, could not escape the test of freedom. In order to assert himself, to become an individual, he distanced himself from the Father, like the prodigal son of the parable. Hence, the world created from nothing—that is having of itself no foundation—began to slide toward nothingness, the nothingness to which we ourselves and the fallen angels, whom we tend to forget, give a destructive consistency. In a certain sense God has been excluded from his creation and only maintains it from without. God has become a "king without a city" to borrow a phrase from a great Byzantine spiritual master of the fourteenth century, Nicholas Cabasilas. In the presence of universal evil—the world that "lies with evil," as John said—"the face of God streams with blood in the shadows," to use the violent phrase of Léon Bloy, often cited by Nicholas Berdiaev.

Until the yes of one woman, which permitted the excluded God to enter once again into the heart of creation in order to rescue humankind from fatality and from the fascination with non-being and to open up, through the darkness, the path of resurrection. But the Crucified God does not have a power of a tyrant or a storm. It is an immense inflow of peace, of light and love which, in order to be effective, needs people to open themselves freely to God. The Parousia will come about as a breaking through. Already there is no moment which cannot allow this light to pass, but there needs to be some preparation: in Christ, under the breath of the Spirit, humanity discovers once again its vocation as *created creator*. Faced with the man born blind, Jesus rejected all explanations based on sin. Neither this man nor his parents had sinned. But this meeting was for the glory of God, and so Jesus healed him. The spirituality of the third millennium will be less one of denial than one of transfiguration—an Easter spirituality, *a spirituality of resurrection!*

Then we will understand that one cannot place limits on hope, as Hans Urs von Balthasar has written, following the great seventh-century mystic Isaac the Syrian. Prayer and work for universal salvation will be the response to the tragedy of hell. Hell as a general condition, as the absence of God, was destroyed on Holy Saturday, and since then there has been nowhere from which God is absent. But it is necessary to "sit at the table of sinners," as Thérèse of Lisieux said, and "pour out blood from the heart," as Silouan, the holy staretz of Mount Athos maintained, so that the final hell, that of the individual walled in on himself might be washed in the waves of love from the communion of saints, these sinners who have accepted pardon.

One of tomorrow's most important spiritual foundations will thus appear as *kenosis*. As Paul said in his Letter to the Philippians, God, or rather God in Christ, *ekenosen*, emptied himself. A truly inspired intuition: to evoke God not in the language of fullness but in that of emptiness. Fullness suggests riches, abundance, power. Self-emptying, emptiness expresses the entire mystery of love. God moves toward humanity in a reverse movement: it is not an over-full God, who would overwhelm humanity, but a God "emptied" and awaiting our response of love.

## Accepting Responsibility for the Spiritual Unity of the Planet

The unity of the planet is in the process of becoming a reality despite increasing counter pressure from the search for local identity. It seems to me that there are two great divisions that will characterize the spiritual condition of humanity today and tomorrow. The first division is between two spiritual hemispheres. The first stems from India. Hinduism, Jainism, and all the various forms of Buddhism (some of which, in China and Japan, live side by side with archaic traditions such as Shinto), or like Buddhism itself or Taoism, come from what Karl Jaspers called the "axial period" of history (8th–6th century BC). In this hemisphere the divine—or the breath of life, the Chinese *chi*—is everywhere apparent, the impersonal divine which the world manifests and in which the world is reabsorbed. The dominant idea is an all-encompassing Unity, Sameness, the universality of the Self and a cyclic understanding of time. (One of the Upanishads asks why does a mother love her child. The response: it is not for love of the child but for love of the Self, which of course is the same in each.)

One could call the other hemisphere "semitic." Today it embraces chiefly Judaism and Islam (at least in their exoteric forms). Here, there is a strong sense of a personal God and of the person as individual. There is a strong idea of *the other—without unity* (except in certain forms of Sufism and Kabbalism marked by neoplatonism). God gives a law and humanity must obey it. Time is linear, whether in tension as in Judaism or in memory as in Islam.

The other division places traditional societies in opposition to modern western society. Traditional societies are superstitious or magical; they hold on to old ways and are often profoundly vitalistic, as we see in Africa and South America. Whereas modern western society is humanistic, innovative, and not vitalistic. Today it is sweeping around the globe, but traces of the traditional societies survive, along with a deep nostalgia, and their magic nourishes the "New Age."

The spiritual foundations of the future, in this context, are the Trinity and divinized humanity.

Certainly in the short term we must affirm above all that our God is not a God of "holy wars" and crusades, but the God of the life-giving cross. Differences, even contradictions between religions should not be an occasion for war, but rather for friendship and prayer, if not shared at least together, as at Assisi. Moreover, these exchanges can immensely enrich Christianity, for in an eschatological perspective, it must be recognized that God's ways are many and various.

More profoundly, we need to understand and spread ever more widely the mystery of the triune God. The living God is so *one* that he bears within himself the reality, the pulsation of the *other* and, in the Spirit, in the holy Breath, overcomes all duality not by collapsing into an impersonal unity, but by a *coincidence of absolute unity and absolute diversity*. And the same is true of humanity, at least on the level of promise, seed, becoming, since the human being is made in the image of God: total unity in Christ, total diversity in the flames of the perpetual Pentecost. A Russian priest and monk was a missionary in Siberia at the dawn of the Revolution. He wrote that he admired the Buddhist monks so greatly that he hesitated to baptize them. But, he added, these wise men were so absorbed in their own inwardness that their eyes were closed. The mission of Christians could be to bring them to open their eyes and to see *the other* without in any degree forsaking this interiority, some of whose paths they can open up for us.

The other fundamental theme for the future is divinized humanity, which is the space of the Spirit and of creative freedom. All the eastern experiences of the divine and all the western experiences of what it is to be human could find a place in the divinization of humanity. To those religions which emphasize transcendence, we would speak—doubtless through their mystical traditions—of the incarnation and *kenosis* (emptying). To those religions which stress fusion with the impersonal, we would speak of the triune God. We would remind the more or less atheistic humanisms that human beings would be nothing if they were not, beyond all their conditioning, an enigma, a mystery which we enter only through the revelation of love.

Then we will be able to respond to present expectations concerning the cosmos, *eros*, transformative meditation, which are gradually crystallizing in the new age movements and which will become anti-Christian if we do not learn how to understand them.

Plutarch recounts how a great cry had resounded across the seas: "The great Pan is dead!" It seems he has been reborn today. We become aware of our bodies as we bring them into harmony with the rhythms of the cosmos. In central Europe, the ecological movement unites with Buddhism in a desire to dissolve back into nature, the immense, maternal *Gaia*.

There is no doubt that the future of Christianity lies in the rediscovery of a mystical and liturgical vision of the cosmos. The eucharist fulfills the sacramental potential of matter. It is the role of us humans, the priests of the world, to offer to God, in the great Christic sacrifice of reintegration, the spiritual essence of created things. It is up to us to give to this transforming vision the widest possible cultural and social scope and to use it to fertilize ecological concerns. The great Russian wisdom figures attempted this at the beginning of the century. Their ways of thinking were certainly awkward, but we will have to take up once again their meditation on Wisdom—this mysterious figure who appears above all in Proverbs 8 and in whom God and creation seem to mutually interpenetrate. Through wisdom, the ancient myths of the Sacred Earth can be integrated into Christianity in a poetic of communion. And most certainly there is a link between Wisdom and the Mother of God in whom the Earth at last discovers its face.

Secondly, it must be noted that, in the history of Christianity the mistrust of *eros* was for a long time necessary in order to uphold the full significance of the person and especially of the woman as person, against the biological determinism and ecstatic union. Gradually, however, *eros* had come to be less transfigured than denied outright; hence, the present-day revolt of life, which has unleashed itself with some extravagance. A renewed Christianity will discover the full meaning of *eros*. It will point to its fulfillment through art, which offers a first draft of the transfigured world, and through ascesis, which renders both man and woman "separate from all and united to all," as Evagrius Ponticus used to say. It will respect the wildest passion closing its eyes to its blind alleys, knowing that those who live and die by such a passion are marked with a seal of the absolute. It will celebrate truly personal love, the poor, great and noble love between a man and a woman, when *eros* is part of an encounter of persons and when the "ecstasy of life" becomes the most powerful language a man and a woman can speak. But this is not to forget that only monastic life can fully realize the marriage of Christ to the soul, and that it is a blessing laid on the spirituality of marriage, the mystery of children.

Thirdly, the question of transformative meditation. Many experience today a great need for silence and peace. People are looking to India and especially to Buddhism for methods of concentration. They sometimes attain a certain detachment and inner unification. But they are imperilled by gnostic pride and the swollen ego that they confuse with the oriental Self. They also risk confusing the general fatigue of today's West with Buddhist negation of desire.

The Christian challenge for tomorrow will be to rediscover and actualize the tremendous spiritual heritage of Christianity. I am thinking particularly—way beyond the various emotional and psychological expressions of "mysticism"—of the great Orthodox tradition of the *Philokalia* (a word that means love of Beauty) and of hesychasm (from *hesychia*—referring to peace, and the silence of union with God). This is a tradition, moreover, that has its roots in the rich soil of the undivided Church. Hesychasm is aware of techniques similar to those of Asia, ways of freeing oneself of mental idols, cleansing the mind of "thoughts," uniting the mind and the heart, using the rhythms of the body such as the breath or the heartbeat. At this level a dialogue is possible. But it seems to me that the Hindu (or Buddhist) often (but not always) merges in a negative sense with the luminous abyss of the Self, or in that "nirvana." Whereas the hesychast discovers that this light flows from a personal source, at once very near, yet always "beyond." Meditation, then, becomes a relationship in which unity is inseparable from otherness, and it culminates in communion with God and neighbor: that service of one's neighbor which has always been, for western Christianity, both a need and a reality.

## A New Way of Life

The modern age has wanted to make Christianity a "religion," that is to say, an intellectual system wrapped in sentimentality and, in the East, with ritualism. We are discovering that Christianity pervades every aspect of existence, that it is the revelation and communication of Life. The Christianity of tomorrow will not simply be one compartment in our culture but will serve to interrogate and vitalize this fundament, this paradigm in which social and political realities are rooted. Christianity as a minority religion will have a greater outreach for being post-ideological and post-sociological, and in it baptism, confirmation, and eucharist will resume their full stature as initiation to Life, neither exoteric nor esoteric, but a Mystery unveiled and for that very reason more mysterious. There will be learned people among these Christians, people whose learning is inseparable from the difficult work of spiritual transformation, and capable of throwing light upon the complexity of humanity at large and the cosmos. Then the words of Ignatius of Antioch will make sense, "true knowledge of God is Jesus Christ."

Gradually the Church will reveal more clearly its vocation: not merely an institution, not simply an assembly of believers, but the mystery of Life, a place of rebirth, where the heart's depths can be opened. It will be a place of prayer (not to invite God in, he who is closer to us than we are to ourselves, but to open ourselves to his presence), a place where prayer will overcome narcissism, where communion, made more or less conscious, can overcome individualism, but also where one might apprentice oneself to contemplative solitude, the source of all creation.

Christians will speak less of love, less of the other, more of self-acceptance (love your neighbor *as yourself*) of discretion and respect, of the self-emptying (kenotic) capacity to give oneself over to every life so that all life may grow. They will prefer *auctoritas* (authority—from *augere*, to cause to grow in freedom) to the constraint of *potestas* (power). The inevitable violence that accompanies individuation, instead of being blandly overlooked, will acquire the virtue of strength through asceticism, creativity, beauty and play.

Masculine and feminine will appear as two ways, equally honorable, of bringing both humanity and the universe into full existence. A renewed symbolism beyond the current mish-mash will allow liturgical play to be renewed as well. Christ is the complete human being in whose nuptial chastity masculine and feminine are equally assumed.

In a new historical context the Spirit will give full scope to the three-fold dignity of the Christian as priest, prophet, and king.

King, therefore life's warrior and peacemaker in one. King through mastery and influence. I am thinking of those statues of the Buddha—the Awakened One—with one hand pushing back, the other receiving. But there is no king without a fool. This wholly inward kingship will make room for folly to keep things in perspective and to bemuse. At the heart of this world's culture the Beatitudes will define a counter-culture, the culture of a world turned inside out. The destiny of the king will be one of irony.

Priest for the world, after the age-old understanding of the great Jewish spiritual masters: a minority in a population can only attain to universality by assuming a priestly role. For such a priest the entire world is a church. His goal as monk will not be to create a society of the pure but to act as leaven at the very heart of an impure society. The lay person will enjoy a monasticism of the heart. The scientist will not be a reductionist, but one who respects. The artist, who at times explores the abyss but also celebrates the "fire of things" and the "icon of faces," will be someone who celebrates the eucharist in all things, as Paul asked.

As prophet he will announce, indeed anticipate, the kingdom where God will be "all in all" (God already is, but it is a mystery in both senses: hidden and sacramental). He will smash idols and open up new paths; outrun Freud in allowing the immense "Song of Songs" of the universe to have all its dimensions, the highest of which is mystical; outstrip Nietzsche by announcing "the God who dances" while trampling down death and hell, wrestling with Adam and Eve from the disintegration of nothingness, as in the frescoes of the *parecclesion* of Chora in Constantinople.

The Christianity of tomorrow, more than ever, will find itself between divine humanism and martyrdom.

1493